MW01275539

Passing the
PMI Scheduling Professional
(PMI-SP)® Certification Exam the
First Time!

Daniel C. Yeomans, PMI-SP, PMI-RMP, PMI-PMP,
PMI-ACP, CSM, CSPO, CMQ/OE

Contributor: Peter Rogers, MA, MMA

This edition published by
Dog Ear Publishing
4010 W. 86th Street, Ste H
Indianapolis, IN 46268

www.dogearpublishing.net

ISBN: 978-145755-663-0
This book is printed on acid-free paper.

Printed in the United States of America

This book is dedicated to my friends, students, and associates at Northwest University, Green River College, and Bellevue College who provided valued input, ideas, and support. You inspire!

Contents

Contents

Preface

Project Time Management is a challenging area that can make or break a project, yet over 50% of all projects fail to meet original scheduling objectives.[1] This book expands upon five domains developed by the Project Management Institute (PMI) comprising content from the PMI Scheduling Professional (PMI-SP) Certification Exam.

The PMI-SP certification was developed to acknowledge expertise of project managers and practitioners as they develop project schedule strategy; develop and implement scheduling planning documentation; monitor and control schedule status; close out schedules; and communicate effectively with key stakeholders. Quoting from www.pmi.org:,

> Schedules are a fundamental element of project management yet half of all projects — 50 percent — are not completed within the initially scheduled timeframe, according to our 2015 Pulse of the Profession® report. Projects and teams today are increasingly global and virtual, and project schedules are key to managing activities, resources, dependencies, and ultimately, project outcomes. The PMI-SP will recognize your knowledge and skill to drive the improved management of project schedules.

This book is designed for project managers and other professionals who may or may not want to attain PMI-SP certification. It defines a proven Time Management Process and includes activities and practice test questions to help you achieve the goal of passing the certification examination the first time. I am confident your individual abilities to plan and manage project schedules will be enhanced through your studies.

Good luck on the PMI-SP Certification Exam, should that be your goal. If you only use this book to improve your schedule management skill set, I salute you! The desire to take your project management skills to a deeper level in the area of schedule management is admirable. Study hard, prepare, and pass the test the first time!

Daniel C. Yeomans

---

[1] www.pmi.org (Certifications)

Foreword

A project schedule is basically a model – like any model, if the inputs are wrong – the conclusions are wrong.

Don't be discouraged by the Introduction. Project scheduling is a combination of art and science. It is much more than an intricate roadmap for how a project will be delivered. In order to develop a realistic and flexible project schedule, a PM must draw from most of the fundamental and advanced skills required to skillfully deliver a complex project. Stakeholders are identified and managed, and project team members get their first exposure to how the PM responds to schedule input. Is the PM autocratic? Does the PM encourage others to participate in building, reviewing, and adjusting the project schedule? How the PM works with all stakeholders to develop the schedule sets the tone for the work environment, beginning with setting the level of commitment and accountability from the people who will deliver the work. Your PM success begins with a solid schedule based on input and shared ownership from your team – this book is an excellent place to start.

A successful project manager for over 35 years, Daniel C. Yeomans has delivered comprehensive project management training all over the world, beginning with his experience in the US Air Force. Dan is a college professor, corporate trainer, author, and independent consultant who holds numerous certifications in every aspect of project management, including Scheduling, Risk, and Quality Management. Over the years, Dan provided "hands-on" training, consulting, and coaching for countless project managers in classrooms, conference rooms, and boardrooms. Dan is a very special teacher with a unique and memorable delivery – his students remark his approach to training keeps the material fresh and easy to recall.

I have been managing projects for over 25 years, from implementing Treasury systems managing over \$50B to implementing Global Security Operations Centers, to building one of the top 5 most visited websites in the world. I can always count on Dan as a world-class resource to provide me with valuable guidance and direction. He is one of a kind.

As an author, you will see that Dan does not borrow from Shakespeare. Dan does not waste the reader's time. Instead, his style is all about easy access to information – all of his books on project management have a personal voice that conveys information easily. They are valuable table-side reference materials for a host of necessary project management skills.

Dan's project management "viewpoint" is based on solid, tried-and-true principles – he is not trying to re-invent the wheel in this book.   Instead, he succeeds in breaking down key lessons in a way that can be easily consumed and used by the reader. How do you start building your schedule?   How does a PM account for unknowns? How do I implement Change Management, and what does that mean? The purpose of this best-of-breed book is to help project managers solve problems and achieve certification, for those who seek it.

A project schedule is outdated as soon as it reaches the printer. Consider the schedule as a living document.

Any schedule you build requires ongoing care and feeding to monitor and control progression. This book provides a valuable resource on project scheduling and covers all the necessary components, from developing a Schedule Strategy to stakeholder communication to implementing formal Change Management. In my early formative days learning to be a project manager – like many other PMs, I struggled with the questions easily explained in this book – I'm only sorry it was not available some 25 years ago. To those aspiring project managers who seek certification or aim to add a few new tools to your toolbox, I enthusiastically endorse this book for your project management career growth and success.

D. Alex Wright, Microsoft--Symetra

Project Manager – Consultant – Coach – Trainer

About the Author

Daniel C. Yeomans became a Project Manager in 1977 while serving in the United States Air Force. Since that time, he has successfully coached, mentored, and trained thousands of Project Managers in a variety of settings.

Dan holds a Master's Degree in Business Administration (MBA) from St. Martin's University in Olympia, Washington. He is certified by PMI as a Project Management Professional (PMP), Scheduling Professional (SP), Agile Certified Practitioner (ACP), and Risk Management Professional (RMP). He is also recognized as a Certified ScrumMaster (CSM), Certified Scrum Product Owner (CSPO) and Certified Manager of Quality/Organizational Excellence (CMQ/OE). He also completed training to become an Emergenetics Associate.

Dan is a member of the Project Management Institute (PMI) and the local PMI Puget Sound Chapter. He also uses his skills to support a number of non-profit organizations, including the Air Force Sergeants Association (AFSA).

Dan is currently working as an adjunct professor at Northwest University in Kirkland, Washington, supporting the institute's undergraduate- and graduate-level business programs. He is also a corporate trainer for Bellevue College and Green River College. His primary focus includes the project management and financial management curriculum areas. He also works as an independent consultant for P17 Group in the Seattle, Washington, area.

Dan developed more than 100 specific training offerings at both university and corporate levels. He developed a benchmark course and workbook for PMP certification that enabled hundreds at the university and corporate levels to successfully attain PMP or CAPM certification. He has a track record of success and seeks to share his successes with others using this book as a guide.

About the Contributor

Peter Rogers

Peter Rogers combines a strong academic background with his high-impact development expertise to bring out the best in people, their teams, and their organizations. Peter challenges people to choose what and where they want to be and enables them to thrive in the ecosystems that they influence and mold to their purposes. Peter draws heavily from his advanced degrees in biological and management sciences, policy, and economics as he works with people to frame solutions to the most daunting challenges.

Drawing on over 30 years of experience, with over 20 of those years as a consultant to Microsoft and other Fortune 100 companies, Peter typically works with leaders and managers in the space between strategy development and strategy implementation to assure that organizations allocate their resources to the work that will deliver on their goals and strategies. He assures that leaders' visions resonate with those who are asked to deliver on those visions and causes unproductive behaviors and work to be replaced with productive behaviors and work.

Prior to forming P17 Group, Peter was instrumental in the startup and success of two companies. In a third company, Cell Therapeutics, he served as head of strategic projects and helped to take this company public on NASDAQ. Peter has been an adjunct professor and guest lecturer at Florida International University and several other colleges and universities. He has spoken at Project World and other conferences.

Peter actively seeks opportunity and is an advocate of the importance of change, risk, and adventure. He is an avid sailboat racer and finds that being of service, particularly helping others to go where they want to go, brings the most meaning to his life.

Contact: Peter@p17group.com

Introduction

Thank you for purchasing *Passing the PMI Scheduling Professional (PMI-SP)® Certification Exam the First Time!* This edition covers all domains and study references for the current test. The goal of this book is preparing you to pass the PMI-SP Certification Exam the first time. I am confident this book will give you greater insight into project scheduling best practices.

PMI-SP is one of many certifications offered through PMI. Once achieved, this certification places you above the rest in terms of scheduling competency. The concepts covered in this book are appropriate for effective scheduling management in project and non-project environments.

This book uses three key references as source documents:

1. *Project Management Body of Knowledge (PMBOK),*[2] 5th Edition. Covers key project management concepts at a high level. Although the primary focus of *this* book is scheduling, it is highly advisable that PMI-SP candidates have a basic understanding of project management principles in the *PMBOK*.

2. *Practice Standard for Scheduling*[3]. Resource published by PMI. **Note**: Information covered on the actual certification exam extends beyond the information in this publication.

3. *PMI Scheduling Professional (PMI-SP) Exam Content Outline*[4]. Lists key objectives covered in the PMI-SP Certification Exam. This book maps to those objectives.

---

[2] Project Management Body of Knowledge, 5th Edition
[3] Practice Standard for Scheduling, 2012 Edition
[4] PMI Scheduling Professional Exam Content Outline, 2012 Edition

Objectives

This book supplements the PMI Time Management Process defined in the 5th edition of the *PMBOK*. We are confident you will gain a far greater understanding of a proven process to schedule projects effectively by reading this book. The PMI Time Management Process defines key tools and techniques that can be applied to projects, which improves overall scheduling skills. In this edition, you have access to a:

- series of activities designed to prepare you for the PMI-SP Certification Exam. We encourage you to complete each activity. Activity solutions are in Appendix A.

- 150-question "final test" to check your readiness to challenge the examination. The test covers key scheduling objectives stated in PMI literature. It also covers questions in other areas of project management you may encounter on the test.

- list of acronyms. Acronyms are often used on the certification exam in place of the written-out definition, so they must be understood. For example, WBS is more commonly used instead of spelling out Work Breakdown Structure. Acronyms are in Appendix C.

- comprehensive glossary of terms used for reference. The glossary is in Appendix D.

- *italicized* entries for are important concepts that often appear on the certification exam.

Key concepts are repeated more than once throughout this book. This is by design. Repetition enhances understanding and learning.

- We include excerpts from the book's contributor, Peter Rogers. Peter adds his ideas and thoughts based on many years of real-world experience. Project scheduling is critical to every project, whether or not you are certified.

The PMI Scheduling Professional Certification Exam

The PMI-SP Body of Knowledge includes five key areas, or domains, and the PMI-SP Certification Exam covers all of them. An in-depth understanding of scheduling activities supporting each domain is critical to pass the certification exam.

Five Domains of Project Scheduling Management

1. **Schedule Strategy**: This area includes 14% of all questions. Five tasks in the Schedule Strategy domain include:

Tasks	Domain 1: Schedule Strategy Tasks
1.	Establish project scheduling configuration management policies and procedures, incorporating best practices, regulations, governing standards and organizational policies, and procedures, to ensure accessibility, storage, retrieval, maintenance, change control, and baseline change control.
2.	Develop schedule approach, based on unique characteristics of the project, including enterprise environmental factors and organizational process assets, in order to define schedule requirements.
3.	Establish scheduling policies and procedures regarding methodology, selection of a scheduling tool, scheduling parameters, performance thresholds, activity granularity, presentation format, earned value management (EVM) implementation, analysis techniques, and approval requirements by using resources such as organizational process assets and project documents in order to develop the schedule management plan and standardize operational procedures.
4.	Develop the schedule-related components for project management plans (for example, integration, scope, cost, quality, resources, communication, risk, and procurement management) through review of contract requirements, in order to integrate scheduling activities into the overall project management process.
5.	Provide information about project scheduling and goals, the role of the scheduler, and scheduling procedures to project team members to facilitate effective participation in the project.

2. **Schedule Planning and Development**: The Schedule Planning and Development domain includes 31% of questions and concentrates on multiple *PMBOK* areas. Twelve tasks are in this domain.

Tasks	Domain 2: Schedule Planning and Development Tasks
1.	Develop work breakdown structure (WBS), organizational breakdown structure (OBS), control accounts (CA), and work packages through communications with subject matter experts and stakeholders and analysis of contractual commitments in order to ensure completion of the project scope.

2.	Define activities and milestones through communications and subject matter experts, decomposition, and application of scheduling policy and procedures to identify and document the work to be performed.
3.	Estimate activity durations, utilizing subject matter experts and scheduling techniques such as three point, parametric, analogous, and/or Program Evaluation and Review Technique (PERT) in order to develop an overall schedule model.
4.	Sequence activities, incorporating defined dependencies (internal, external, and cross programs, milestones, and constraints (for example, calendars, geography, contracts), in order to develop a logical, dynamic schedule model.
5.	Identify critical and near critical path(s) using techniques such as Critical Path Method, Critical Chain, Program Evaluation and Review Technique (PERT) and Monte Carlo simulation in order to meet project delivery date requirements .
6.	Develop the project resource breakdown structure (RBS), determine resource availability, and assign resources to activities by working with functional managers, project managers, and project team members in order to define the resource constrained schedule.
7.	Adjust schedule model based on resource availability, available budget, and other known constraints in order to calculate the resource constrained schedule.
8.	Align schedule with overall program plan or integrated master plan (IMP), through review of enterprise objectives and contract documentation, in order to ensure accomplishment of overall program objectives.
9.	Analyze major milestones against statement of work (SOW), the contract, and/or memorandum of understanding, to assess whether schedule model delivery estimates meet required deadlines.
10.	Perform schedule risk analysis using quantitative tools or techniques (for example what if scenarios, Monte Carlo simulation) in order to determine if project milestones are achievable within acceptable risk tolerances.
11.	Obtain a consensus of the project customer, sponsor, project manager, and project team members, in order to establish an approved project baseline.
12.	Establish the performance measurement baseline (PMB) using organizational processes and standard techniques, in order to enable performance measurement and management.

3. **Schedule Monitoring and Controlling:** The Schedule Monitoring and Controlling domain includes 35% of all questions. Six tasks are in this domain.

Tasks	Domain 3: Schedule Monitoring and Controlling Tasks
1.	Collect activity status at defined intervals from the activity owners via reports, meetings, inspections, or other standard procedures in order to update and review the project progress.
2.	Collect resources information and updates via reports, timesheets, meetings, inspections, or other standard procedures in order to report on resource utilization and availability.
3.	Perform schedule analysis and audit, on in-house and subcontractor schedules, using industry standards, guidelines and best practices in order to identify and report project schedule, status, changes, impacts, or issues.
4.	Identify alternative project execution options, using tools and techniques such as what-if-scenario analysis, in order to optimize the schedule.
5.	Incorporate approved risk mitigation activities into the schedule, by utilizing defined change control processes, in order to establish a new performance measurement baseline (PMB).
6.	Update the schedule model and document schedule baseline changes, received through formal change control processes, in order to maintain and accurate schedule and facilitate forensic schedule analysis if required.

4. **Schedule Closeout:** This domain includes 6% of all questions. Five tasks are in this domain.

Tasks	Domain 4: Schedule Closeout Tasks
1.	Obtain final acceptance of the contractual schedule components, by working with sponsor and/or customer, in order to facilitate project closeout.
2.	Evaluate final schedule performance against baseline schedule, scheduling approach and implementation, using standard scheduling tools and techniques, including solicitation of feedback from stakeholders, in order to identify lessons learned and develop best practices.
3.	Update the organizational process assets, through documentation of identified lessons learned and best practices, in order to improve business processes.

4.	Distribute final schedule reports, including earned value management (EVM) calculations and variance analysis, to stakeholders in order to facilitate project closeout.
5.	Archive schedule files (for example, final schedule model, schedule management plan, periodic status reports, schedule change log), as per defined procedures in order to satisfy contractual requirements and prepare for potential forensic schedule analysis.

5. **Stakeholder Communications Management**: This domain includes 14% questions. Four tasks are in this domain.

Tasks	Domain 5: Stakeholder Communications Management
1.	Develop and foster relationships with project stakeholders, consistent with the communications management plan, in order to enhance support for the project schedule.
2.	Generate and maintain visibility of the project schedule, by working with the project manager and/or stakeholders, in order to maintain stakeholder support.
3.	Provide senior management and other stakeholders with verbal and written schedule status updates and impact on schedule of corrective actions, as defined by the communications management plan, in order to maintain stakeholder awareness.
4.	Communicate schedule issues that could impact delivery of project scope or adherence to the schedule management plan, in order to elevate awareness to relevant stakeholders.

Qualifications for Testing

You must complete an application through PMI to qualify for the PMI-SP Certification Exam[5]. You may also complete a paper or online application. The application must show you have adequate education and experience in the scheduling management area of project management to qualify to take the test.

The PMI-SP certification is a stand-alone credential. It is administered in English only. You may take the test up to three times in a one-year period to attain a passing score. The ability to test is not impacted by other PMI certifications you may possess.

The table below provides an overview of required education and experience needed to qualify for testing:

Table A.1 PMI-SP Education and Experience Requirements

Education	Project Scheduling Experience	Project Scheduling Management Education
Secondary diploma (high school diploma, associate's degree, or global equivalent)	At least 5,000 hours spent in the specialized area of professional project scheduling within the last 5 consecutive years	40 contact hours of formal education in the specialized area of project scheduling (includes scheduling tools training as well)
OR		
Four-year degree (bachelor's degree or global equivalent)	At least 3,500 hours spent in the specialized area of professional project scheduling within the last 5 consecutive years	30 contact hours of formal education in the specialized area of project scheduling

---

[5] www.pmi.org

About the Test

You are authorized to take the PMI-SP Certification Exam after your application is approved by PMI. Listed below are specifics describing the certification exam process.

- Test is computerized. All questions are multiple-choice, with four potential answers. Each question has only one correct answer. Most test questions are short and straight forward. Some include extraneous verbiage designed to distract. Always try to understand what the question is asking before responding.

- Write down notes before you start the test. Take advantage of a 15-minute tutorial on how to use the computerized testing system. You are provided pencils and notepaper or equivalent to use during the test. This tutorial should not take more than a few minutes to complete. Take advantage of time remaining to write down key pieces of information before you begin the actual test. Consider the following topics, at a minimum.

  - scheduling models

  - inputs, tools and techniques, and outputs for all Project Time Management activities

  - formulas such as Earned Value Management (EVM), Program Evaluation and Review Technique (PERT), etc.

  - definitions you may wish to reference during the test

- The test is 170 questions, and 150 questions are graded. Another 20 questions are "pre-release" and are not graded. You cannot identify pre-release questions. Answer all questions to the best of your ability.

- You have 3.5 hours to complete the test. You have the option to mark questions you want to review before you finalize the test.

  - Go through the test one time and answer questions you are sure of first. Then go back to answer the more difficult questions. You can mark questions to review later.

  - Take a periodic break during the test. Many professionals recommend a short break every 50 questions to catch your breath and refresh yourself.

- Testing is conducted at designated testing centers. You schedule your testing time at the center of your choice after your application is approved.

- A calculator is provided for math questions. You are provided a handheld calculator or one embedded on the computer.

- Have two picture IDs when you arrive at the testing center. A locker is provided for you to store personal items.

- PMI has not published a passing score for the PMI-SP credential. Strive for a 75% score on all practice tests in this book.

- You are notified of your pass/fail status at the completion of the exam. You are given a scorecard showing proficiency levels in each of the five PMI-SP domains. **Note:** You can score a "Below Proficient" in one or two areas and still pass the test.

- You are required to attain 30 Professional Development Units, or PDUs, over a three-year period to maintain the certification after you pass the test.

Note: Should you have any questions, please contact me at Dan@P17Group.com.

Chapter 1: Introduction to Project Scheduling

Project scheduling is a critical component essential to success of a project. The key goal of the Project Scheduler is to apply learned skills, applicable techniques, and scheduling tools to develop appropriate schedule models. Figure 1.1 provides a visual of schedule modeling methodology and key components. Welcome to our introductory chapter.

Schedule Modeling

Figure 1.1 Schedule Modeling and Key Components

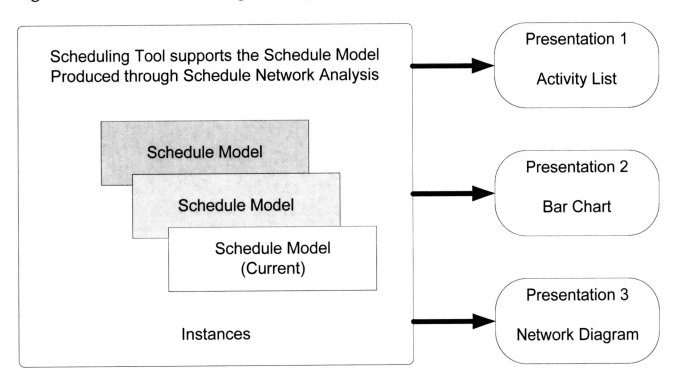

Let's explore this figure. Knowledge of these components helps immensely on the certification exam.

- **Schedule Network Analysis**: The Project Scheduler performs schedule network analysis at the beginning of schedule planning. This produces a schedule model using various techniques covered later in this book, such as Critical Path Method (CPM), Critical Chain Method, What-If Analysis, etc. Selection of scheduling tools, models, and presentations are included in the Schedule Management Plan, a key concept addressed later.

- **Scheduling Tool**: One of the first decisions a scheduler needs to make is selecting a scheduling tool. Scheduling tools are *automated* applications that perform schedule network analysis that generate instances of a project schedule. Microsoft Project, Excel, etc., are common scheduling tools. Each scheduling tool has a unique Project Schedule ID to identify the project it supports and differentiate from other schedule models.

- **Schedule Model**: Schedule models are a dynamic representation of the plan for executing project activities. It applies selected scheduling methods and uses the scheduling tool to produce various schedule model copies, referred to as *instances*.

- **Instances:** Instances are copies of the schedule model. Multiple instances are completed as the project progresses and the schedule model changes. Instances provide a variety of *presentations*, such as critical path analysis, resource data, activities started and completed, etc. Always annotate the "Project Version." This is the revision number, version code, or "as of date" used to identify currency of the instance.

- **Presentations:** Presentations are specific outputs from the schedule model used to communicate data used for analysis, course correction, decision making, etc. Figure 1.1 shares common schedule presentations, including activity lists, bar charts, and network diagrams.

Schedule Modeling is critical to the project.

- **Scope**: The Work Breakdown Structure (WBS) lists required activities that must be completed to satisfy project needs. A schedule model must accommodate all activities, acknowledge dependencies, and ensure project objectives are met. In addition, a schedule model needs to account for events occurring on other projects impacting your project.

- **Resource Utilization and Planning**: Schedules impact resources. An activity that requires five days of effort at 100% utilization must be scheduled differently if a 50% utilization rate is the reality. Ensure the right people are in the right place at the right time.

- **Risk**: Scheduling risk is real. Effective schedule models allow schedulers to identify and prioritize risks impacting project completion milestones. Schedule models also define risk at a level allowing What-If Analysis, should issues develop.

- **Earned Value Management (EVM)**: Effective schedule models allow for measurement of Earned Value (EV) and Planned Value (PV), allowing key status and forecasting requirements to be met. EVM is covered extensively in later chapters.

Project Scheduling Creation Process

Schedule creation is a step-by-step critical process. Figure 1.2 provides an overview.

Figure 1.2 Project Scheduling Creation Process

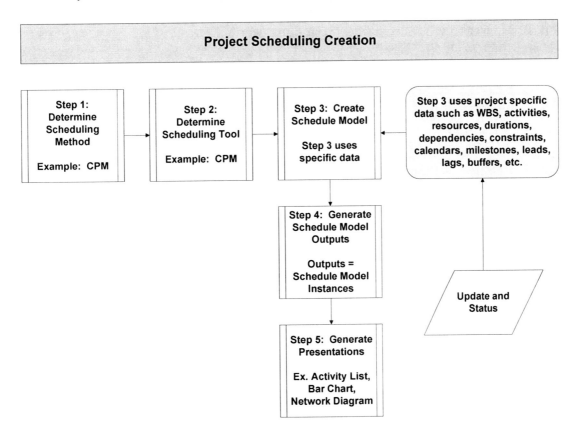

- **Step 1: Determine Scheduling Method**: Select the appropriate scheduling method. The most common choices are defined in this chapter. They include Critical Path Method (CPM), Precedence Diagramming Method (PDM), and Critical Chain Method.

- **Step 2: Determine Scheduling Tool:** There are a variety of scheduling tools. Oftentimes, companies have a pre-determined tool of choice. Microsoft Project is a common scheduling tool used by many. Other organizations may develop hybrid scheduling tools to suit their needs.

- **Step 3: Create the Schedule Model:** Effective scheduling depends upon other project management functions. Effective scheduling models are only as good as data you input. Project specific data as the WBS, well-defined activities, required resources, realistic durations, dependencies, constraints, project calendars, critical milestones, leads; lags, buffers, etc. should be input for the model to be effective.

- **Step 4: Generate Schedule Model Outputs:** Multiple instances, or schedule model outputs, are generated throughout the course of a project. Determine a rhythm for when, how, and to whom instances will be presented.

- **Step 5: Generate Presentations:** Presentations are shared on a periodic basis. Define the type of presentations, when they are shared, and to whom they are shared in the Project Communications Management Plan. We discuss this plan later. Presentations continue to be updated and shared as the progress progresses to a hopeful successful conclusion.

Scheduling Methods

Numerous scheduling methods may support your project. Knowledge of these models helps you select the most appropriate for your project. Most common methods include Critical Path Method (CPM), Precedence Diagramming Method (PDM), Critical Chain Method, Rolling Wave Planning, and Activity Diagramming Method (ADM).

Critical Path Method (CPM)

CPM allows you to determine three critical scheduling attributes. First, it allows you to determine total duration of the project and the earliest possible finish date. Second, it allows you to determine activities on critical path, and which are not. Activities not on critical path provide scheduling flexibility referred to as float. Finally, CPM enables determination of early start and early finish dates by applying a forward pass, and late start and finish dates by applying a backward pass. These concepts are discussed in more detail later. CPM is the prevalent method used in modern scheduling tools.

Figure 1.3 depicts a project activity or Work Package using CPM.

Figure 1.3 CPM Activity Node

There are seven distinct sections depicted on a CPM Activity Node.

- **Early Start (ES):** This is the earliest an activity can start. In the example, this activity can start on Day 1.

- **Early Finish (EF):** This is the earliest an activity can finish. In this example, this activity can finish on Day 3. The ES and EF can be calculated using a method called the *Forward Pass*.

- **Duration (D):** Duration represents the amount of time in hours, days, weeks, etc. that an activity requires to complete. Determine a standardized duration such as days, weeks, etc. for each project. The timeframe selected is defined in the Schedule Management Plan.

- **Activity Name:** Each project activity requires a distinct name. In this example, we named activity "A" for simplicity. However, in a real-word environment, each activity should be described by using an action-result methodology. For example, "Develop Checklist".

- **Late Start (LS):** This is the latest the activity can start. In the example, the latest this activity can start is Day 1.

- **Late Finish (LF):** This is the latest an activity can finish. In this example, this activity can finish no later than Day 3. The LS and LF can be calculated using a method called the *Backward Pass*.

- **Float (F):** Float is a measure of the difference between the ES and LS, and EF and LF. In the example, there is no difference between these dates. Therefore, this activity has 0 float. Any activity with 0 float is on the critical path.

Precedence Diagramming Method (PDM)

PDM is an approach that supplements CPM. PDM and CPM partner to provide a project network diagram showing required project activities, durations, and allows a determination of the Schedule Baseline through critical path analysis. Figure 1.4 provides an example of a CPM model using PDM. It is a critical model essential for managing the schedule component of any project.

Figure 1.4 CPM Using PDM Model

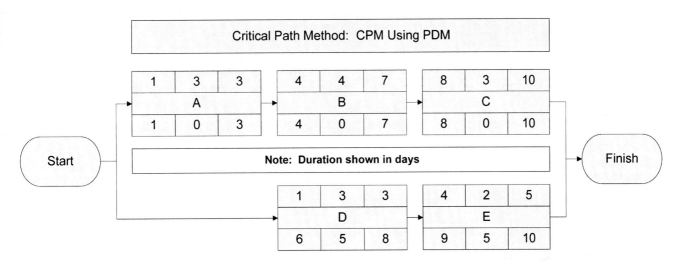

There are five activities in this model.

- *Critical path* is the path of longest duration. There are two paths. Path ABC is 10 days. Path DE requires 5 days. Therefore, critical path for this model is 10 days. Critical path is the amount of time a project requires to complete.

- The *float* for activities on path DE is 5 days. Calculate by comparing ES with LS, and EF with LF. Using Activity D, ES is 1 day, and LS is 6 days. This is a difference of 5 days, which equals float. EF is 3 days, and LF is 8 days. Again, a difference of 5 days. The difference between ES and LS, and EF and LF, should always be the same within an activity. If not, recheck the math.

Critical Chain Method

Critical Chain Method is developed from the CPM approach and considers the impact of uncertainties or risk on the project. Critical Chain Method can be used to consider resource constraints, mandatory delays, or inclusion of other safety margins required to successfully manage a schedule baseline. Critical Chain Method uses *buffers* to show points in the project network diagram where delays or additional time or resources are required.

Figure 1.5 features three types of Critical Chain Methods using a variety of buffer types. These include project buffers, feeding buffers, and resource buffers.

Figure 1.5 Critical Chain Methods

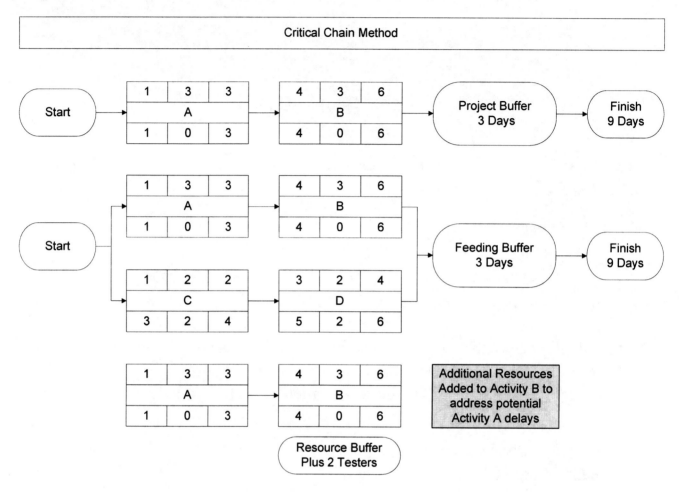

Here is a quick overview of three types of buffers.

- **Project Buffer:** Project buffers are added between the final project activity and project planned completion date. Project buffers add time to the end of the project to account for a variety of uncertainties identified during project planning.

- **Feeding Buffer:** Feeding buffers are added at the merger point of the critical and non-critical path. They, too, consider uncertainties identified during project planning.

- **Resource Buffer:** Resource buffers are not depicted on the project network diagram. Instead, they are acknowledged on the project RBS as additional resources required to complete a project activity due to uncertainties identified during planning. In the example shown, resources for Activity B would be applied to help complete Activity A in the event of unforeseen delays. The RBS is discussed in detail later.

Rolling Wave Planning

Rolling Wave planning is a method where you plan in detail activities known and understood, and delay planning on successor activities until more information is understood. This method is "plan as you go." Figure 1.6 shows how Rolling Wave Planning works. A more detailed explanation follows.

Figure 1.6 Rolling Wave Planning

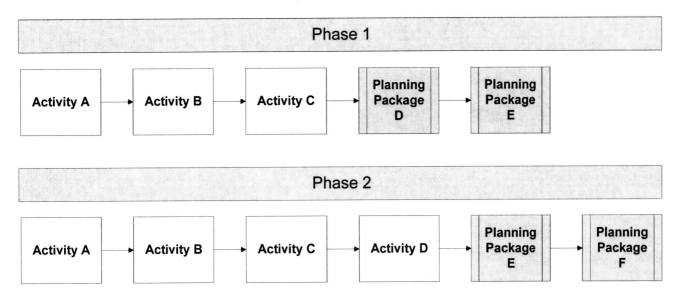

During Phase 1, Activities A, B, and C are planned in detail. Activities D and E are planned at a high level and are referred to as *planning packages*. In Phase 2, Activity D is planned in detail based on learnings from executing Activities A through C. Planning package F was added at the end of Phase 2.

Arrow Diagramming Method (ADM)

The final model is the Arrow Diagramming Method, or ADM. This method is also named Activity on Arrow (AOA) method. ADM is used for scheduling activities in a project plan. Precedence relationships between activities are represented by circles connected by one or more arrows. The length of the arrow represents the duration of the relevant activity. *ADM only shows finish-to-start relationships'*, meaning each activity is completed before the successor activity starts.

Sometimes a dummy task is added, to represent a dependency between tasks. This is not any actual activity. The dummy task is added to indicate precedence that can't be expressed using only actual activities. A dummy task has a completion time of 0.[6] Figure 1.7 shares an example of an ADM/AOA network diagram.

Figure 1.7 ADM/AOA Diagram

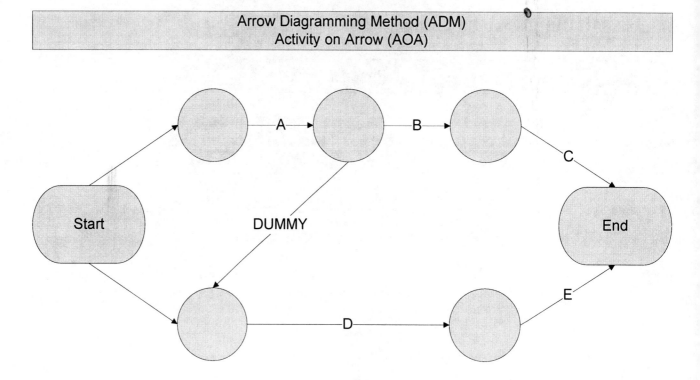

Agile Methodology

Agile methodology is similar to Rolling Wave Planning. Agile focuses on achieving useable results quickly. Key concepts regarding Agile include:

- **Iterations:** Traditional Waterfall methods develop a Scope Statement and build to the plan. Agile uses an iterative approach. At the iteration end, the plan is adjusted to adopt change and meet the needs of the customer.

---

[6] Wikipedia

- **Iteration Planning:** In Scrum, iterations are referred to as Sprints. *Agile uses a form of CPM planning* to determine what is produced in a given Sprint.

- **Product Backlog:** Requirements are documented in a Product Backlog with User Stories. The backlog is updated, or groomed or refined, at the completion of an iteration, or Sprint. User Stories are reprioritized and updated.

- **User Stories:** User Stories state the role (customer), need, and value proposition. In addition, they define acceptance criteria.

- **Deliverables:** Agile strives to produce some increment of value by the end of a Sprint. Formal demonstrations are provided to customers at the conclusion of the Sprint.

- **Retrospectives:** Retrospectives replace Lessons Learned. Retrospectives evaluate performance of the team and strive to define and implement improvements.

- **Adaptive:** Agile is referred to as an *adaptive* project management methodology. Waterfall uses a *predictive*—or build to the plan—methodology.

Chapter 1 Summary

This chapter introduced key schedule modeling concepts needed to pass the PMI-SP Certification Exam. As a project manager, understand these models, and choose those most appropriate for managing your project. The goal of a project manager is to deliver every project on-time, within budget, and provide scope that meets requirements and is fit for use. As the Project Scheduler, your job is ensuring the on-time component is met. Over 50% of projects fail to meet required schedules[7], but these models and knowledge of how to use them can help you be successful.

Chapter 2 discusses the Schedule Strategy domain. This chapter shares key concepts in establishing a schedule approach to help ensure project success.

Activity 1 provides a number of key concepts with definitions. Use this activity as a means of ensuring you understand concepts shared in this chapter. Responses are in Appendix A.

[7] www.pmi.org/certifications

Activity 1: Introduction to Project Scheduling

Directions: Match the scenario or definition to potential responses provided.

Introduction to Project Scheduling Activity	Response
1. Activities planned at high-level pending information needed to plan them later in greater detail as the project progresses.	
2. The path with the longest total duration on a project network diagram. Duration depicts total time required to complete a project.	
3. The documents that contains requirements in the form of User Stories used in Agile Project Management.	
4. Uses buffers to show points in the project network diagram where delays or additional time or resources are required.	
5. The prevalent method used in modern scheduling tools. Allows you to calculate total duration, critical path, and early start and early finish dates.	
6. A method where you plan in detail activities that are known and understood and delay planning on successor activities until more information is understood.	
7. Specific outputs from a schedule model used to communicate key data to be used for analysis, course correction, decision making, etc.	
8. Acknowledged on the project Resource Breakdown Structure as additional resources required to complete a project activity due to uncertainties.	
9. Add time to the end of the project to account for a variety of uncertainties that may be identified while planning a project.	
10. Copy of a schedule model. Provide a variety of presentations such as critical path analysis, resource data, and activities started and completed, etc.	
11. Dynamic representation of a plan for executing project activities. Applies a selected scheduling method and uses the scheduling tool.	
12. Normally an automated application that helps perform schedule network analysis to generate instances of a project schedule.	
13. Used for scheduling activities in a project plan. Precedence relationships between activities are represented by circles connected by one or more arrows.	
14. Define the role, need, and value proposition. Additionally, outline acceptance criteria necessary for the team to attain.	

Activity 1: Choose from following:

A. Rolling Wave Planning

B. Resource Buffer

C. Critical Chain Method

D. Scheduling Tool

E. Arrow Diagramming Method (ADM)

F. Planning Package

G. Presentation

H. Instance

I. Critical Path Method (CPM)

J. Critical Path

K. Schedule Model

L. Project Buffer

M. Product Backlog

N. User Story

Chapter 2: Schedule Strategy

W. Edwards Deming perfected the work of Walter A. Shewart and developed the Plan, Do, Check, and Act (PDCA) concept that drives project management methodology today. Schedule Strategy development is the first planning activity the Project Scheduler must perform. This chapter shares key concepts essential to developing and documenting a Schedule Management Plan, schedule approach, acknowledges key policies and procedures impacting the approach you select, and provides a roadmap to help achieve scheduling objectives and goals.

Schedule Management Plan

The first planning step in Project Time Management is development of a Schedule Management Plan. This plan is a process driven "how to" guide defining applicable scheduling methods as CPM, schedule tools, and details of the schedule model including required presentations. This plan establishes and shares applicable policies and procedures necessary to plan, execute, control, and manage the project schedule throughout the project's lifecycle.

Schedule Management Plan Inputs

There are a number of inputs required to accomplish the Schedule Management Plan.

- **Project Management Plan:** Documentation in the Project Management Plan is essential to review early in schedule planning. Information available is likely limited to the Stakeholder Management Plan discussed in Chapter 6, and Scope Baseline which includes the Project Scope Statement, Work Breakdown Structure (WBS), and WBS Dictionary discussed in this chapter. Documentation impacting cost, quality, human resources, communications, risk, and procurement is added later. Each of these areas impact the schedule.

- **Project Charter:** The Project Charter is the initial document authorizing a project to enter the planning stage. The Project Charter link to Schedule Strategy and planning is defined later.

- **Enterprise Environmental Factors:** Some factors may constrain schedule planning. These factors are essential to understand as you identify schedule models, tools, etc. Learn more about Enterprise Environmental Factors later in this chapter.

- **Organizational Process Assets**: Most organizations have established ways of doing business. The Project Scheduler needs to conform to these methods to be successful. Learn more about Organizational Process Assets later in this chapter.

Schedule Management Plan Tools and Techniques

The Project Scheduler leads the Schedule Management Plan development process. There are three distinct tools and techniques defined by PMI to assist in this process.

- **Expert Judgement:** I use a statement quite often to explain Expert Judgement. "Know what you know, know what you don't know, and surround yourself with people who know what you don't know." It takes a team to be successful. Surround yourselves with those who can help you be successful—don't work in a vacuum.

- **Meetings:** Meetings can be a blessing or a curse. When facilitated correctly, meetings add value and provide information needed to create and implement the schedule model discussed in the next section. Learn effective meeting management and maximize the time you spend with stakeholders.

- **Analytical Techniques:** Understand all moving parts of the project and how they impact the project schedule. Estimation techniques, project management information system selection, scheduling methodology and more must be considered. Success of the Schedule Management Plan can be summarized in two ways. First, all stakeholders have a common understanding of how the schedule will be planned and managed. Second, they are committed to support the process.

- **Project Management Information Systems:** Technology can help manage schedules. Choose the technology best meeting the needs of the project.

Schedule Management Plan Outputs

General areas are addressed in a Schedule Management Plan. Figure 2.1 addresses these areas:

Figure 2.1 Schedule Management Plan Content

Component	Content
Schedule Model Development and Process Descriptions	• Schedule model and tools • Schedule model creation process • Key stakeholders involved in schedule model creation process — roles and responsibilities
Level of Accuracy	• How estimation is accomplished • How contingencies are addressed
Units of Measures	• Project estimation: hours, days, weeks, etc. • Other measures team needs to be aware of
Organizational Procedures Links	• Schedule interaction with other project management processes • Pointers to key documentation such as the WBS • How project documents are stored and archived
Project Schedule Maintenance and Reporting Formats	• How schedule status is documented and shared • Specific presentations required for various stakeholders
Control Thresholds	• Areas of variation to be measured • Specific variation thresholds acceptable and unacceptable • How to address variances
Performance Measurement	• How success is measured • Stakeholders needing measures
Configuration Management	• How schedule change requests are evaluated and processed • Who approves various change requests

Creating a Schedule Model

Creation of an appropriate schedule model to meet project needs is responsibility of the Project Scheduler. Figure 2.2 provides a proven step-by-step approach. Schedule model creation specifics for your project are defined in the Schedule Management Plan. There are many key concepts to understand to successful develop and implement this model.

Figure 2.2 Schedule Model Creation

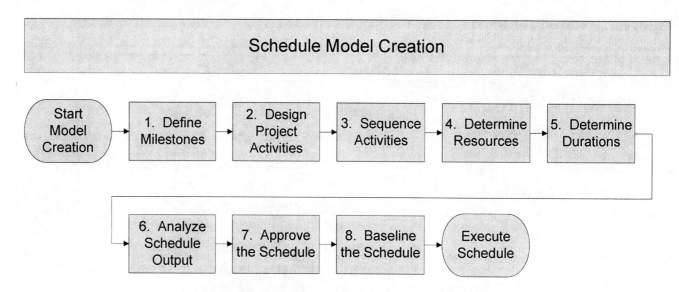

Key activities and decisions required during each step of this eight-step process:

- **Step 1: Define Milestones:** *Milestones* are key events or points in time that must be met to achieve project goals and objectives. Milestones have no duration or resources assigned. They are used as benchmarks to measure progress, and may occur at the beginning, mid-point, or end of the project. Oftentimes milestones are tied to the start or completion of key project deliverables. *Deliverables* are defined as any tangible, measureable output the project produces. Deliverables generally are key product or service attributes to satisfy project goals and objectives.

- **Step 2: Design Project Activities:** A project activity is any unit of work that must be accomplished to ensure a project is successfully completed. A great tool to define project activities is a *Work Breakdown Structure (WBS).* A complete WBS is essential to success of this step. A WBS ensures all required activities are identified and documented. In addition, each activity identified in the WBS should satisfy (SMART) guidelines:

  o **Specific:** Each activity requires a specific action and result. For example, "Install carpet." Each project team member should have a like interpretation of the action and result required. Eliminate ambiguity or confusion on specific objectives of the activity before proceeding.

o **Measurable:** Each activity should be measurable in terms of time, cost, resources required, etc. You need to answer the question "What does success look like?"

o **Achievable:** Ensure activities can be assigned to a single member of the project team commits to ownership of the activity and is responsible for completion. As part of this analysis, verify capacity and skill sets.

o **Relevant:** Activities should provide value to meet the stated scope for the project in the Project Charter, Scope Statement, etc. If not, consider eliminating the activity.

o **Target Driven:** Activities should be completed in an uninterrupted fashion with consideration given to dependencies. *A normal rule of thumb is that any given activity should be broken down to complete in a timeframe that is less than half of your normal reporting cycle.* For example, if a reporting cycle is two-weeks, schedule activity durations of one-week or less when possible. This allows the Project Scheduler to make adjustments during the current reporting cycle and seek assistance if needed.

• **Step 3: Sequence Activities:** Successful completion of Step 2 allows completion of Step 3. Sequencing activities results in a *project network diagram* showing activity relationships, dependencies, and allows for eventual calculation of critical path and creation of the Schedule Baseline. Refer back to Figure 1.4. This figure showed a network diagram for a small project of four activities. Some activities can be started sequentially. Other activities are dependent upon completion of predecessor activities. This book provides elaborates on the sequence activities step in Chapter 3.

• **Step 4: Determine Resources:** Resources are people, materials, supplies, and equipment required to implement the project. Project resource requirements and constraints are generally defined in the project *Resource Breakdown Structure* detailed in Chapter 3. Initial considerations to develop a schedule model:

o What resources are required? A best practice is reviewing specific resources required for each project activity and aggregating total project requirements.

o Do constraints limit your options? For example, do labor laws limit the time an external resource can work?

o Is resource availability an issue? For example, if a specific piece of test equipment only available at certain times, you must arrange the schedule around the availability.

o How available are personnel resources? For example, if a team member is responsible to complete an activity in 20 hours, determine the time this resource is available each day before determining the final activity duration. If the resource is available for 5 hours a day, plan for 4 days. However, if the resource is available only 4 hours a day, plan duration of 5 days. The *Productivity Index* of resources is defined later in this chapter.

- **Step 5: Determine Durations:** The Project Scheduler determines realistic durations for each activity in the WBS. There are estimation techniques to leverage during this step. In Chapter 3, we share estimation techniques as analogous, parametric, bottom up, and Three-Point. Some additional food for thought:

  o Avoid "One-Point" estimation unless you have a high degree of confidence in the single estimate you plan to use. A "One-Point" estimate has a probability of approximately 15% of being correct. These are not great odds.

  o Determine a standardized duration measure for consistency. Mixing hours, days, and weeks can be confusing and lead to scheduling errors.

  o Ensure activity owners are qualified to provide duration estimates. The sum of all activity durations results in finalization of your Schedule Baseline.

- **Step 6: Analyze Schedule Output:** Two key objectives are accomplished in this step. First, ensure the schedule model provides information and detail needed by the team to complete the project successfully? Second, ensure the sequence of all activities make sense? Identify dependencies and ensure schedule flow is logical.

o Most schedule models use a scheduling tool to automate the schedule analysis and calculations. Ensure the scheduling tool you select meets the needs of the project.

o Ensure start and finish milestones are connected. Ensure all activities can be traced from beginning to end. All activities must have a clear input(s) and clear output(s). *Open ended activities* lack a predecessor, successor activity or both. Open ended activities obscure logical relationships between activities, create a false picture of potential float, and reduce the potential to identify and document risks.

• **Step 7: Approve the Schedule:** The schedule must be *approved and accepted* to be officially designated as the Schedule Baseline.

o *Approval* authority of the final schedule rests with the Project Sponsor. Keep the sponsor informed as the schedule is being developed and share issues needing resolution. The Project Scheduler manages expectations to avoid last minute surprises.

o Schedule *acceptance* must be received from key stakeholders and the team. Include the team in schedule development and gain their commitment each step along the way. Share key scheduling objectives and goals to attain participation and commitment. In the end, you need a committed team to implement the project schedule to achieve success. Include the team early and often—ensure the team looks upon the schedule as "ours" versus "theirs."

• **Step 8: Baseline the Schedule:** The last step in the schedule model creation process is to capture the finalized and agreed upon schedule. This schedule becomes the baseline upon which future performance is measured.

o Schedule Baseline status and other required reports are communicated on a regular basis in the project *Communications Management Plan*. This plan is discussed in later chapters.

o The ONLY way to change the Schedule Baseline is to process an approved change through the Integrated Change Control process. The original baseline is maintained for reference and comparison.

o **Note:** The *Schedule Baseline* is the approved and accepted schedule documented in the Project Management Plan.

Schedule Strategy and the Project Charter

The Project Charter is the first formal document accomplished when a project is born. The Project Charter is approved by the Project Sponsor and authorizes the project manager to begin detailed planning to include the schedule. The Project Charter defines the summary milestone schedule driving more detailed schedule planning efforts. The Project Charter also defines project approval requirements, and other factors impacting the schedule. Approval of the Project Charter is referred to as *pre-baseline*. The Project Charter:

- Provides authority for the project manager to begin schedule planning. It authorizes use of resources needed to effectively develop a project schedule. Finally, the Project Charter defines sponsorship for the project.

- Can be initiated by a Business Case, Statement of Work, and/or an agreement. It is critical the Project Scheduler be aware of information in these documents as they impact the schedule.

- Provides key contract requirements, regulations, and governing standards impacting the project schedule. The Project Scheduler must be aware of these requirements when planning the project schedule.

- Acts as a key input to the Schedule Management Plan highlighted earlier in this chapter.

Configuration Management

Configuration management is a set of formal procedures used to identify, document, and manage the *functional and physical characteristics* of a project. The project's functional and physical characteristics are impacted by both the project schedule and budget. Configuration management is implemented through a Configuration Management Plan. This plan defines items that can be configured, those requiring a formal change control process, and instructions to identify, record, verify, and audit changes. Formal schedule control processes should define baseline control, status update procedures, variance thresholds, etc.

Project Schedulers establish configuration management policies and procedures to safeguard the schedule baseline. Use of Lessons Learned and best practices should be incorporated into project plans to enable success. Regulations, governing standards, and organizational policy must be considered. Schedule model and data accessibility, storage, retrieval, maintenance, and change control must be defined to support the Schedule Baseline.

Schedule Strategy Approach Considerations

There are factors to consider when developing a Schedule Strategy. Here are considerations impacting the schedule model.

- **Organizational Process Assets:** Considerations include organizational policies and procedures, standard project management tools and templates, and historical information as Lessons Learned. Considering Organizational Process Assets allows the Project Scheduler to ensure conformance to corporate standards, and develop schedule models consistent with best practices used in the organization.

  - A key Organizational Process Asset is the **Organizational Breakdown Structure (OBS).** The OBS is a hierarchical organizational chart depicting the top-down organizational model for the firm. The Project Scheduler must know where potential team members are working, develop relationships with Functional Managers managing resources needed on the project, and be aware of various advantages and disadvantages posed by various organizational structures.

- **Enterprise Environmental Factors:** Considerations include acknowledgement of the organization's structure, systems, and culture. Standards and regulations impacting your project are additional Enterprise Environmental Factors to consider. Enterprise Environmental Factors can act as *constraints*—realities dictating what you can and cannot do in terms of project scheduling.

- **Scheduling Tool Selection:** Many organizations use standard scheduling tools. Tools availability and choices are generally included in corporate Organizational Process Assets. When choosing a tool, ensure the tool performs all necessary functions. These functions may include, but are not limited to:

  o **Scheduling Parameters**: The tool selected must support the length of the project, and provide types of presentations required by both management and other select project stakeholders in the format required.

  o **Performance Measurement:** The tool must be capable of measuring planned versus actual performance, and reporting status in a manner supporting the needs of multiple stakeholders. A common measurement method is EVM, which is discussed in detail in Chapter 4.

  o **Activity Granularity:** The project manager decomposes the project WBS to a level of granularity that fits the needs of the project. A Work Package is defined as the lowest level of detail. Work Packages must be estimable, be assignable, and provide value. The scheduling tool selected must support the level of detail required to effectively schedule and manage the project.

  o **Analysis:** An effective scheduling tool allows for adequate levels of *variance analysis* so the Project Scheduler can review planned versus actual progress, identify problems early, and identify root causes.

- **Schedule Integration:** The project schedule is impacted by many project planning components. Components include integration, scope, cost, quality, human resources, communications, risk, procurement, and stakeholder management functions. The project schedule is impacted by other activities and cannot be built in a vacuum.

Schedule Strategy and the WBS

The WBS is a key document created prior to the initiation of in-depth schedule planning. It is a *hierarchical decomposition of the total project scope* required to produce a required product or service. The schedule planner must understand this document and use it for schedule planning. Figure 2.3 provides a sample WBS. Note the various components that are important when planning the project schedule.

Figure 2.3 WBS Example

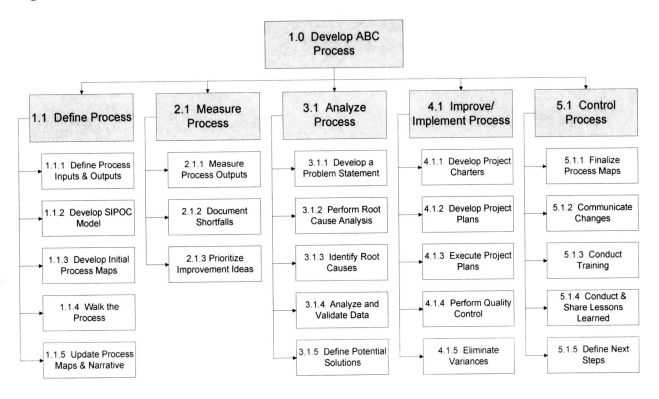

The WBS defines all activities necessary to accomplish the project in relative order of accomplishment. Some clarifications:

- **WBS Hierarchy**: Build the WBS from top to bottom. Each activity has a distinct identifier called a *Code of Account Identifier*. The project level is Level 1 and designated as Activity 1.0. The Phase is Level 2. Note this example uses the DMAIC model. Each Level 2 activity is designated as a two-number identifier. Level 3 activities are designated by a three-number identifier. Some WBS models may use a different numbering system. If so, no problem. Ensure each activity has a unique number for reference.

- **Chronological Order**: Strive to build the WBS in a manner showing the order that activities must be implemented. At Level 2, Activity 1.1 occurs before Activity 2.1. At Level 3, Activity 1.1.1 occurs before Activity 1.1.2.

- **Work Package:** The lowest level of a WBS is referred to as a Work Package. Each Work Package needs to be assignable. The process of breaking the WBS down from Level 1 to Level 3 or lower is called *decomposition.*

- **KISS:** This acronym spells out "Keep it Short and Sweet." When possible, try to group like tasks within a single activity. For example, Work Package 1.1.1 in the example states "Define Process Inputs and Outputs." This is actually a multi-task process to complete this Work Package. The fewer Work Packages you have, the greater the utility of the WBS becomes as a planning tool. Document multiple tasks in an activity in a WBS Dictionary (next section).

- **Action-Result:** Note each activity (Levels 1 and 2) and Work Package (Level 3) is annotated using action and result verbiage. Each activity and Work Package needs to be actionable and pass the SMART test shared earlier.

The Work Breakdown Structure (WBS) Dictionary

We encourage you to keep the WBS simple. A WBS Dictionary allows you to describe the details or attributes of each Work Package without adding additional complexity to the WBS. It is also easier to update and maintain than the actual WBS itself.

Figure 2.4 provides a WBS Dictionary format using the DMAIC WBS example in Figure 2.3. For simplicity, we only share the "Define" Phase.

Figure 2.4 WBS Dictionary Example

WBS Dictionary Example		
WBS Identifier	Activity Attributes	References
1.1.1	1. Meet with customer—ensure key process outputs are defined specifically. 2. Inventory current inputs required to support outputs. Define sources.	• FY2016 Customer Satisfaction (CSAT) Report
1.1.2	1. Map out initial process requirements. 2. Trace from Supplier-Inputs-Process Activities-Outputs-Customers. (SIPOC) 3. Process maps MUST address all SIPOC criteria.	• Six Sigma Memory Jogger II
1.1.3	1. Map in Visio. 2. Use basic flowchart types. 3. Map using swim lanes.	• See swim lane examples for vendor management process on SharePoint
1.1.4	1. Schedule one hour meet with process team and customer representative. 2. Walk through the process. 3. Document gaps, omissions, non-value add activities, and questions.	• Stakeholder Register and RACI designations
1.1.5	1. Update initial process maps. 2. Ensure all issues discovered in 1.1.4 are addressed. 3. Assemble process measurement team.	• Stakeholder Register and RACI designations
	Note: RACI = (Responsible, Accountable, Consult, Inform)	

The concept behind the WBS Dictionary is logical. Reference each Work Package by the Code of Account Identifier. Then describe the Work Package attributes. Many WBS Dictionaries provide actual links to references in the body of the document. To repeat a key point—add details in the WBS Dictionary and keep your actual WBS simple. The WBS and WBS Dictionary are shared together.

Productivity Index

Project Schedulers must know which team members are responsible for completing project activities and acknowledge skill sets and availability vary. The Productivity Index concept helps you on the certification test, as well as plan realistic schedule durations in a real-world environment. Figure 2.5 shares a Productivity Index Overview for four team members.

Figure 2.5 Productivity Index Overview

Productivity Index				
Team Member	A	B	C	D
Skill/Efficiency Level	1	0.5	0.8	0.5
Availability	100%	100%	50%	60%
Productivity Index	1.00	0.50	0.40	0.30
Solutions	(1 x 1)	(0.5 x 1)	(0.8 x 0.5)	(0.5 x 0.6)
Individual Time to Complete 3 Day Activity	3	6	7.5	10.0
Team Members A and B	2	3/(1.0 + 0.5)		
Team Members C and D	4.29	3/(0.4 + 0.3)		
Team Members A, B, C and D	1.36	3/(1.0 + 0.5 + 0.4 + 0.3)		

- **Productivity Index:** Each team member has a Productivity Index rating. This rating is calculated by multiplying the skill/efficiency level times the availability of the team member.

  o Team Member A has the highest skill level and is 100% available. The math: 1 times 100% = Productivity Index of 1.0.

  o Team Member C has a 0.8 skill level. Availability is 50%. The Productivity Index for this member is 0.8 times 50% = 0.4.

- **Individual Times to Complete an Activity:** Let's assume an activity requires three days to complete. Using the Productivity Index, how long would it take each team member to complete the activity, assuming they are working alone?

  o Team Member A has a Productivity Index of 1. Divide the amount of time required to complete the activity by the Productivity Index. In this case, we have 3/1 = 3 days.

  o Team Member C has a Productivity Index of 0.4. Doing the math, we have 3/0.4 = 7.5 days.

- **Combined Team Member Completion:** You can calculate how long an activity will require to complete when combining team members. Divide the activity duration by the combined Productivity Indexes of the team members working on the activity.

o Let's look at the combination of Team Members C and D. The math looks like this: $3/(0.4 + 0.3) = 4.29$ days.

o We can include all four team members as well. Working together, the activity will require $3/(1.0 + 0.5 + 0.4 + 0.3) = 1.36$ days. As you see, the more resources working on an activity — the better.

Chapter 2 Summary

This chapter discussed Domain 1 of the PMI-SP Certification Exam. Developing a Schedule Strategy is critical to later schedule planning.

Following the step-by-step approach to create a schedule model is a proven methodology that yields results. We define each of these steps in detail in Chapter 3. Be aware of the many considerations essential to successful schedule development. Project managers are integrators. It is essential to understand the cause and effect nature of all planning activities, and not plan given functions in a vacuum.

The WBS is the cornerstone of planning. We refer to the WBS as a key planning input as we dig deeper into the planning strategy presented in this chapter. Remember the place to describe the attributes of a Work Package is in the WBS Dictionary.

Not all resources produce equally. The Project Scheduler cannot always assume a human resource will be available 100% of the time and produce at 100% efficiency. The Productivity Index allows for development of a more realistic Schedule Strategy based on skill sets and availability.

Challenge yourself to complete Activity 2. Activity responses are in Appendix A.

Activity 2: Schedule Strategy

Review Chapter 2 and fill in the blanks with the correct term, concept, or definition.

Schedule Strategy Challenge	
Question	Response
1. A hierarchical organizational chart that depicts the top-down organizational model for the firm	
2. Any tangible, measureable output that the project will produce. Generally, key product or service attributes that satisfy project goals and objectives	
3. Hierarchical decomposition of the total project scope required to produce a required product or service	
4. Shows activity relationships and dependencies and allows for eventual calculation of critical path and creation of the Schedule Baseline	
5. Establishes and shares applicable policies and procedures necessary to plan, execute, control, and manage the project schedule throughout the project's lifecycle	
6. Considerations include organizational policies and procedures, standard project management tools and templates, and historical information such as Lessons Learned	
7. Set of formal procedures used to identify, document, and manage the functional and physical characteristics of a project	
8. The process of breaking out project scope from a high level to lower level activities and Work Packages	
9. The process of reviewing planned versus actual progress, identifying problems early, and being able to identify root causes	
10. Allows you to describe the details or attributes of each Work Package without adding additional complexity to the WBS	
11. Key events or points in time that must be met to achieve project goals and objectives. Have no duration and no resources assigned	

12. Tool and technique to surround yourselves with those who can help you successfully plan and execute a project schedule	
13. Initial document that authorizes a project to enter the planning stage approved by Project Sponsor	
14. The unique numeric designator assigned to each activity and Work Package on a WBS	
15. The approved and accepted version of the project schedule included in the Project Management Plan	
16. A numeric designator summing a team members potential work output derived from estimating skill levels and availability	
17. Considerations include acknowledgement of the organization's structure, systems, and culture. In addition, includes standards and regulations potentially impacting a project	
18. Deming perfected the work of Shewart and developed a concept that drives project management methodology today	

Productivity Index Bonus Question	
An activity requires 5 days to complete, assuming a full-time resource with high skill sets. You have assigned a resource that has a skill rating of .75 and an availability of 80%. How long will this resource require to complete the 5-day activity?	

Chapter 3: Schedule Planning and Development

We outlined an eight-step schedule model creation process in Chapter 2. In this chapter we revisit this model at a deeper level. *PMBOK* Chapter 6 shares information to effectively plan a project schedule.

Define Milestones and Design Project Activities

The Define Activities process in the Project Time Management knowledge area allows us to effectively address Steps 1 and 2 in the schedule creation process. See Figure 3.1 as a reference. We review key inputs required to be successful, recommended tools and techniques, and discuss three key outputs essential to success.

Figure 3.1 Schedule Model Creation Excerpt #1

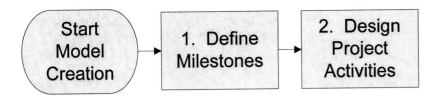

Define Milestones and Design Project Activities Inputs

Inputs necessary to Define Milestones and Project Activities include:

- **Schedule Management Plan:** Prescribes processes required to effectively Define Activities along with the level of detail required to meet specific needs of the project.

- **Scope Baseline:** The Scope Statement, WBS, and WBS Dictionary combine to create the Scope Baseline. Scope planning must be complete before in-depth schedule planning begins. The goal of an effective schedule is to deliver scope as required.

- **Enterprise Environmental Factors:** Consider culture, values, systems in place, standards, regulations, etc., to determine their impact on activity completion and milestone creation.

- **Organizational Process Assets:** Many firms have policy and procedures, standards, templates, etc., required for use by the Project Scheduler. In addition, Lessons Learned and historical information add value to benchmark a project.

Define Milestones and Design Project Activities Tools and Techniques

Tools and techniques allow the Project Scheduler to turn inputs into required outputs to satisfy criteria defined in the first two steps. Tools and techniques supporting Define Activities include:

- **Decomposition:** *Decompose—or break down—the Scope Statement* which is the most detailed version of scope into the activities required to achieve it. Decomposition is also a tool and technique in the Create WBS process which is a precursor to the Define Activities process.

- **Rolling Wave Planning:** Chapter 1 defined the Rolling Wave method of schedule modeling. Define activities considered as planning packages, and define applicable conditional paths, instructions, etc. on what is required before more detailed planning can commence.

- **Expert Judgement:** Define activities as a team. Take advantage of Subject Matter Experts (SMEs) on your team to define activities to the right level.

Define Milestones and Design Project Activities Outputs

Tools and techniques allow development of three specific outputs to satisfy the first two steps of the schedule model creation process. Here is an overview of these two outputs:

- **Step 1: Define Milestones:** Step 1 defines significant points or events in the project. *Milestones are developed and classified as mandated, possibly by a contract or regulatory constraint, or optional based on historical information.* Milestones have no duration and serve as starting and ending points to accomplish key deliverables.

- **Step 2: Design Project Activities**: Two distinct outputs allow the project schedule to successfully achieve Step 2. They include:

  o **Activity List:** Includes all required activities. The Project Scheduler uses the WBS as a guide to determine activities that must be included in the project schedule. Each activity has a unique designator, title, and satisfies the SMART criteria shared earlier.

  o **Activity Attributes:** Each activity is described to a level of detail required for the Project Scheduler to define durations. Activity attributes may include required dependencies, lead and lag options, resource requirements, task assignments, etc.

Sequence Activities

The Sequence Activities process in the Project Time Management knowledge area allows us to effectively address Step 3 in the schedule creation process. See Figure 3.2 as a reference. We review key inputs required to be successful, recommended tools and techniques, and outputs essential to success.

Figure 3.2 Schedule Model Creation Excerpt #2

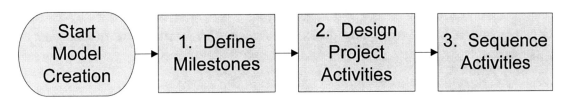

Sequence Activities Inputs

Inputs necessary to effectively Sequence Activities:

- **Schedule Management Plan:** The Schedule Management Plan is a critical document used as an input for *all* schedule planning processes. The Schedule Management Plan prescribes processes required to effectively Sequence Activities along with methods required to complete a project network diagram.

- **Milestone List:** Step 1 provided milestones. Activities must be sequenced in a manner allowing the project to meet milestone forecasts.

- **Activity List:** Step 2 is completed before Step 3. The activity list is reviewed during this step for dependencies, implementation sequences, and is highly dependent upon the quality and completeness of the WBS.

- **Activity Attributes:** Activity attributes must be well defined to provide details and clarity to effectively sequence activities in the order they must occur.

- **Project Scope Statement:** Good concept to repeat--the Project Scope Statement provides the greatest detail of project scope. This detail includes information and data impacting Activity Sequencing.

- **Enterprise Environmental Factors:** Standards, tools, and Work Authorization Systems that impact Activity Sequencing. A *Work Authorization System* is a set of policies, procedures, or rules dictating when you can begin and end new activities. It is in essence a tollgate system requiring validation or approval as you complete each project activity.

- **Organizational Process Assets:** Information included in the Corporate Knowledge Base may dictate specific procedures and guidelines necessary to plan and implement a project schedule.

Sequence Activities Tools and Techniques

Tools and techniques to be aware of when planning the Sequence Activities process:

- **Precedence Diagramming Method (PDM):** PDM was discussed in Chapter 1. PDM has four potential activity relationship types to be aware of.

  o PDM uses terms *successor* and *predecessor* to explain the position of activities. A predecessor activity occurs in sequence prior to a successor activity.

  o PDM—to repeat—is also referred to as AON (Activity on Node) methodology.

o Figure 3.3 outlines four PDM relationship types. Note definitions use predecessor and successor. Familiarize yourself with this terminology.

Figure 3.3 PDM Relationship Types

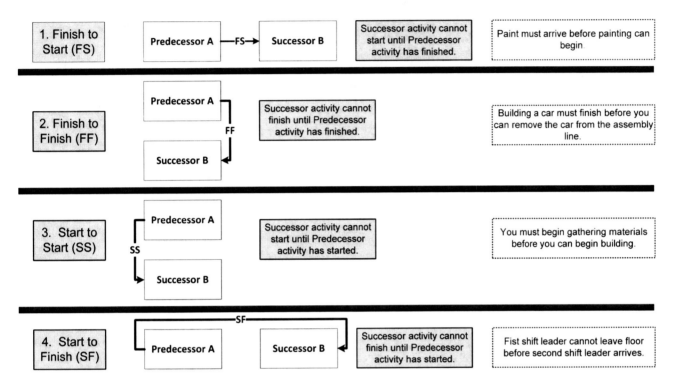

- **Dependency Determinations:** The second tool and technique used in Sequence Activities is Dependency Determinations. There are four types of dependency determinations that determine whether activities are done sequentially, or must be completed in sequence. Figure 3.4 provides an overview.

Figure 3.4 Dependency Determinations

Type	Explanation
Mandatory	Mandatory dependences are created by the nature of the project. For example, you must turn on a server before you can operate it. They are referred to as *hard logic*. Mandatory dependencies are often legally or contractually required or inherent in the work—often involving physical limitations. You may encounter *cross program dependencies* which impact your project that you have no control over. You cannot break mandatory dependencies.
Discretionary	Discretionary dependencies are established based on best practices. For example, it may be best to delay manufacturing until an inventory inspection is complete. You can inventory without inspection, but it may result in problems. These are referred to as *soft or preferred logic*. The primary focus of discretionary dependencies is to reduce risk.
External	External dependencies acknowledge non-project related activities that impact project activities outside control of the team. For example, a new product may not be marketable due to legal/regulatory considerations until the government approves distribution. External dependencies generally involve relationships with project and non-project activities. As with mandatory dependencies, you cannot break an external dependency.
Internal	Internal dependencies are defined as precedence relationships between project activities *within the team's control*. It is possible you could have an "Internal Mandatory" dependency. You may or may not be able to break an internal dependency.

- **Leads and Lags:** Leads and lags are the final tool and technique used in Sequence Activities.

  o **Lead:** Allows a successor activity to begin prior to completion of a predecessor activity.

  o **Lag:** Delays the start of the successor activity even though the predecessor activity may be complete.

  o Figure 3.5 provides a visual to better understand leads and lags.

Figure 3.5 Leads and Lags

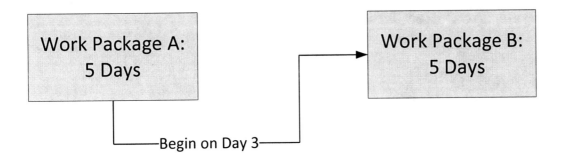

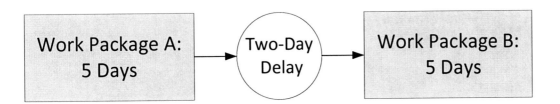

Sequence Activities Outputs

The output of Sequence Activities is a *Project Network Diagram*. Here are some clarifying notes.

- The initial Project Network Diagram does not include time durations. It simply shows the logical flow of all activities based on dependency determinations. This initial Project Network Diagram is referred to as a *Pure Logic Diagram*.

- Try to avoid multiple activities merging at one point. For example, you may have a logic flow requiring Activities A, B, and C to be completed before Activity D begins. Or perhaps Activity D must be completed before Activities E, F, and G can begin. Some term this as a bottleneck. In project management terminology, however, we refer to this as *Path Convergence*. Path Convergence *increases risk*.

- Figure 3.6 shares an example of a Project Network Diagram. We include one instance of Path Convergence and label it accordingly.

Figure 3.6 Pure Logic Project Network Diagram

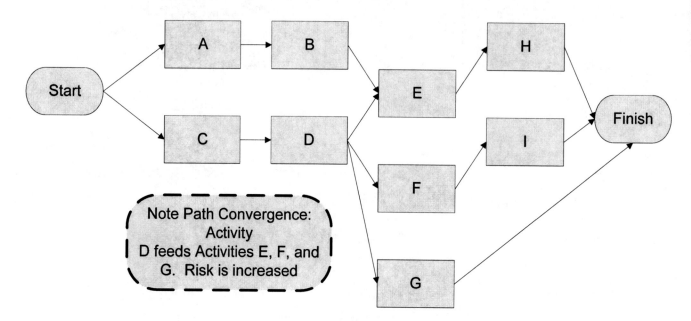

Determine Resources

The Determine Resources process addresses Step 4 in the schedule creation process. See Figure 3.7 for reference. We review key inputs required to be successful, recommended tools and techniques, and outputs essential to success.

Figure 3.7 Schedule Model Creation Excerpt #3

Determine Resources is the fourth schedule model creation step. During this step, a determination is made regarding resources needed in quantities required to perform project activities. Here is a brief list of resources you need to consider as availability, quantity, timing, etc. all impacts the schedule.

- People (internal and external)

- Equipment: Assets subject to depreciation

- Materials and Supplies: Consumables

The Estimate Activity Resources process of Project Time Management addresses key considerations such as when resources are required, where they are needed, and types and categories of essential resources.

Determine Resources Inputs

- **Schedule Management Plan:** The Schedule Management Plan prescribes levels of accuracy, types of resource requirement categories, and more.

- **Activity List and Activity Attributes:** Activities designed and identified in Step 2 serve as a source document for required resources. Review each activity, determine resources, and aggregate total resource requirements. Activity Attributes provide detail and more in-depth definition to ensure you have the right resources at the right time in the right place.

- **Resource Calendars:** Resource Calendars show up on numerous occasions on the certification test. Here is a brief overview of Resource Calendars. They:

  o Share key scheduling considerations such as resource availability, constraints, location and time zones, multi-project tasking, skill sets, etc. They are key in estimating resource utilization.

  o Are an output of the Acquire Project Team process in Project Human Resource Management. Project manager's update resource calendars applicable to their project to include working days, shifts, when and how long resources are required, etc.

o Are not personnel specific. They can also include availability for non-personnel resources such as equipment, supplies and materials, etc.

o Also include contracted resources. The project manager should update organizational resource calendars when contracted resources are identified during the Conduct Procurements process in Project Procurement Management.

- **Risk Register:** The project *Risk Register* is developed as soon as project planning begins. Initial risks identified in the Project Charter are documented in the Risk Register. Risks are added as each planning activity is completed. Resource determinations, durations, dependencies, etc. can all be impacted by risk and must be considered.

- **Activity Cost Estimates:** Time, Cost, and Scope impact each other. Budget availability impacts the number and quality of resources you can acquire during the Determine Resources step.

- **Enterprise Environmental Factors:** Resource location, availability, skill sets, capacity, competing projects, constraints, etc. impact the Determine Resources step.

- **Organizational Process Assets:** There may be standard templates, policies, procedures, etc. to be aware that impact the Determine Resources step. In addition, it is always a great idea to review Lessons Learned and other historical information to benchmark best practices and avoid documented pitfalls.

Determine Resources Tools and Techniques

- **Expert Judgement and Project Management Software:** We repeat a key concept-- project management is a team sport. Use SME for support and guidance. There may be standard software packages used by your organization as part of your Organizational Process Assets. Use these to your advantage.

- **Alternatives Analysis:** Determine the most efficient and effective means to complete the project using resources available. Make or buy, lease, manual or automated, etc. are all considerations to determine the right use of resources.

- **Published Estimating Data:** Some organizations publish cost of resources as part of Organizational Process Assets. For example, an internal manager may be valued at $100 per hour. Cost for using a key piece of testing equipment may be listed as $250 per day. The Project Scheduler analyzes costs to determine the impact on schedules.

- **Bottom-Up Estimating:** The methodology of costing out each activity in the WBS in terms of resources required, then aggregating the results. This method is defined as *Bottom-Up Estimating*.

Determine Resources Output

An output to assist in Determining Requirements is the Resource Breakdown Structure (RBS). The RBS defines total project resource requirements using the WBS as a guide, and allows for determine of needs, gaps, issues, risks, etc. Completion of the RBS may impact earlier project documentation and result in required updates. Figure 3.8 shares an example of an RBS template.

Figure 3.8 Resource Breakdown Structure (RBS)

Resource Breakdown Structure									
WBS Identifier	Human Resources (HR)	Human Resource Attributes	Hours	HR Costs	Materials	Material Costs	Equipment	Equipment Costs	Total Costs
1.1.1									
1.1.2									
1.1.3									
2.1.1									
2.1.2									
TOTAL									

Note 1: The RBS is not a mandatory Project Management Plan entry. In addition, you are encouraged to add or delete columns as applicable that add value to your project. Common additions include:

- Risks

- Issues

- Gaps

- Organizational Identifiers

- Chart of Account Codes (Multiple funding sources)

Note 2: A *Resource Constrained Schedule* dictates scheduling a project based on resource availability. For example, Erika the developer is only able to start Task A on May 12th, so you schedule the task to start on this date.

Schedule Model Creation: Interim Summary

The first four steps of the schedule creation model define key milestones, document required activities, describe how activities must be sequenced based on dependency relationships, and determine resources required to support both the schedule and the project as a whole. We highly encourage you to review *PMBOK* Chapter 6. The Project Time Management knowledge area correlates well with the Schedule Creation Model being highlighted in this chapter.

Activity 3A is an opportunity to review key concepts covered in the first four steps to ensure understanding before moving to Step 5. Match the proper answer to the definition provided.

Activity 3A: Schedule Model Creation Steps 1-4

Schedule Model Creation Steps 1-4 Activity	Response
1. The first step in the schedule model creation process where you determine start and end dates, key points of time where deliverables must be accomplished, etc.	
2. Methodology of costing out each activity in the WBS in terms of resources required and then aggregating the results	
3. Dependences created by the nature of the project. Cannot be broken. They are referred to as *hard logic*	
4. Precedence relationships between project activities that are within the team's control	
5. The approved and accepted Scope Statement, WBS, and WBS Dictionary completed during project scope planning	
6. Defines total project resource requirements using the WBS as a guide, and allows you to determine needs, gaps, issues, risks, etc.	
7. A common method of developing a Project Network Diagram. Also referred to as AON methodology	
8. The process of breaking down the Scope Statement into smaller and more manageable parts through creation of a WBS and WBS Dictionary	
9. The process of beginning a successor activity prior to completion of the predecessor	
10. Critical document used as an input for ALL schedule planning processes. Prescribes processes required to develop the end-to-end schedule	
11. Established based on best practices. They are referred to as *soft or preferred logic*. The primary focus is to reduce risk.	
12. Documents identified risks potentially impacting a project. Identification begins with the Project Charter and doesn't end until all project planning is complete	
13. A document that includes the most detailed version of project scope and drives project activity design efforts	
14. Acknowledge non-project related activities that impact project activities outside control of the team. Often stem from regulations or standards	
15. Successor activity cannot begin until the predecessor activity has begun. A key dependency relationship	

Activity 3A: Choose from following:

A. Scope Baseline

B. Decomposition

C. Define Milestones

D. Scope Statement

E. Schedule Management Plan

F. PDM

G. Start-to-Start

H. Mandatory

I. Risk Register

J. Lead

K. Discretionary Dependency

L. Bottom-Up Estimating

M. Resource Breakdown Structure (RBS)

N. External Dependency

O. Internal Dependency

Determine Durations

The Estimate Activity Durations process in Project Time Management effectively addresses Step 5 in the schedule creation process. See Figure 3.9 for reference. We review required inputs, tools and techniques, and outputs essential to success.

Figure 3.9 Schedule Model Creation Excerpt #4

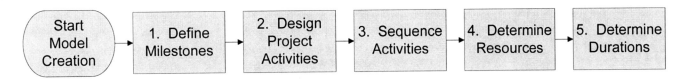

Determine Durations Inputs

Determine Durations is a very challenging step in the Create Schedule Model process. Inputs necessary to Determine Durations are:

- **Schedule Management Plan:** Includes estimation guidance and approved estimation techniques. Provides guidelines for duration accuracy, thresholds, etc.

- **Activity List and Activity Attributes:** You must determine durations for each activity and Work Package identified in the WBS. Activity attributes provide clarifying information on each activity aiding in duration estimation.

- **Activity Resource Requirements:** Use the RBS developed in Step 4. Ensure duration estimates address and accommodate resource constraints.

- **Resource Calendars:** Availability of resources, resource attributes, and capacity can be derived from Resource Calendars.

- **Project Scope Statement:** Assumptions and constraints impacting duration estimation is generally listed in the Project Scope Statement.

- **Risk Register:** Risk impacts duration estimates. There are times when contingency needs to be built into the schedule to avoid or mitigate the potential impact of negative risks.

- **Enterprise Environmental Factors:** Location of team members impacts schedule durations. Virtual teams are more difficult to coordinate. Published data on productivity and duration norms may be available to aid you.

- **Organizational Process Assets:** Historical information to benchmark, Lessons Learned from prior projects, and Resource Calendars mentioned earlier assist in estimating durations.

Determine Durations Tools and Techniques

There are tools and techniques to effectively Determine Durations. One tool discussed on numerous occasions is **Expert Judgement**. We reiterate what we shared—assign the right team members to the right activities. Do your best to assign knowledgeable team members to each activity to provide the best estimates.

- **Estimation Methods:** There are three primary estimation methods to Determine Durations. These methods are not mutually exclusive. You may plan a schedule using all three of these methods for certain activities. Figure 3.10 provides an overview of methodologies.

Figure 3.10 Estimation Methods

Method	Explanation
Analogous (Top Down) (Expert)	• Technique uses actual durations of previous, similarly scheduled activities or entire projects as basis for time estimates • Often called Expert or Top-Down estimating. Most reliable when past projects are similar in fact and not just appearance • **Advantages:** Fast, no need to decompose WBS to a deep level, no need for WBS Dictionary, less costly to create, meets senior management expectations, great for repeating type projects • **Disadvantages:** Less overall cost estimate accuracy, estimates prepared with limited detailed information and understanding, requires considerable expertise and historical data to be successful, difficult for ambiguous projects, can lead to infighting to gain "biggest piece of the pie" , difficult to track planned versus actual project expenditures
Parametric	• Technique quantitatively multiplies quantity of work to be performed × the productivity rate • Uses regression analysis and learning curve techniques • Example: Drawing time is 2 hours × 10 drawings = 20 hours. Look for references to "mathematical" models • Term heuristics refers to "rules of thumb" or generally accepted rules • **Advantages:** Extremely accurate, reduces overall risk, based on historical data, accurate resource quantity and cost data matching • **Disadvantages:** Takes time, may require expensive tools, requires considerable experience to master, difficult for calculating "soft" costs, very difficult for broadly defined or ambiguous projects
Bottom-Up	• Uses WBS as a guide. Each Work Package is individually estimated for time durations and costs • Best for complex and ambiguous projects with many unknowns • **Advantages:** Higher level of accuracy, better team buy-in and commitment, best for complex and difficult to define projects, provides more accurate baseline to track costs and adjust • **Disadvantages:** Takes more time and expenses, team may pad estimates, project must be defined to Work Package level, requires activity ownership, requires greatest level of activity details

- **Three Point Estimation**: It is difficult to determine a single estimation not impacted by risk. Determining a single estimate for activities is defined as *One-Point* estimating. Per PMI, a one-point estimate has an approximate 15% chance of being correct. These odds are not good.

  o Three-Point estimation uses three distinct estimates. You determine an Optimistic estimate, Most-Likely Estimate, and Pessimistic Estimate and use mathematical models to determine the best estimate.

  o Figure 3.11 shows two forms of Three Point estimating. Here is a quick overview of each:

    - **Three Point Averaging:** This form of Three Point sums the three estimates and uses the average to determine the final estimate. The averaging method is also called a *Triangular Distribution.*

    - **Three Point PERT:** *PERT* stands for Program Evaluation and Review Technique. This is a weighted model that uses standard statistical norms that states Optimistic and Pessimistic results occur approximately one out of every six times, and Most Likely results occur approximately four of six times. Note these calculation specifics are constant and never change. PERT is also referred to as a *Beta Distribution.*

Figure 3.11 Three Point Estimation Models

Three Point Estimation			
Estimation Using PERT			
Estimate	Duration	Multiplier	Sub-Total
Pessimistic (P)	38	1	38
Most Likely (ML)	21	4	84
Optimistic (O)	10	1	10
Total		6	132
PERT	Total/6		22.0

Three Point Estimation			
Estimation Using Averaging			
Estimate	Duration	Multiplier	Sub-Total
Pessimistic (P)	38	1	38
Most Likely (ML)	21	1	21
Optimistic (O)	10	1	10
Total		3	69
Average	Total/3		23.0

Formula: (P + (4)ML + O)/6
Referred to as Weighted or Beta Distribution

Formula: (P + ML + O)/3
Referred to as Averaging or Triangular Distribution

- **Group Decision Making Techniques:** There are a number of common group decision making techniques valuable in determining durations. Techniques covered in Chapter 7 include Delphi Technique, Nominal Group Technique, and brainstorming.

- **Reserve Analysis:** There are times when you need contingency reserves or buffers to adjust a schedule for risk. We addressed buffers as a topic of Critical Chain Method in Chapter 1. There are two types of reserves you will encounter on the test—and in the real world of project scheduling.

  o **Contingency Reserves:** Many risks are identified by WBS activity on the Risk Register. These are known risks. Another term used for known risks is "Known Unknowns." *Contingency Reserves* address known unknowns.

  o **Management Reserves:** There are times when project risks cannot be identified until planning progresses, or even project execution begins. These risks are referred to as unknown risks, or unknown unknowns. *Management Reserves* address unknown unknowns.

Determine Durations Outputs

The outputs of Determine Durations are estimates for all activities and potential ranges of possible results. For example, you may develop a 30-day schedule and state thresholds of 30 days +/- 2 days. You may also use probabilities of meeting the schedule. For example, there is a 90% chance of meeting the 30-day schedule objective, meaning there is a 10% chance of missing the 30 day window. We discuss a tool called Monte Carlo later that provides such probabilities.

Analyze Schedule Output

The Develop Schedule process in Project Time Management knowledge area effectively addresses Step 6 in the schedule creation process, and prepares for approval and creation of the Schedule Baseline defined in Steps 7 and 8. See Figure 3.12. We review required inputs, tools and techniques, and outputs essential to success.

Figure 3.12 Schedule Model Creation Excerpt #5

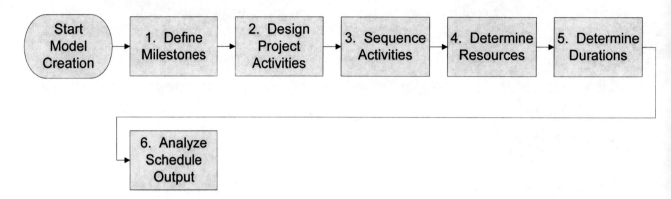

Analyze Schedule Inputs

All outputs from the previous five steps need to be reviewed, validated, and analyzed to ensure they meet the needs of the project. These outputs serve as key inputs to the Analyze Schedule Output step. Here is a list of key inputs:

- Schedule Management Plan

- Milestone List (Step 1)

- Activity List and Activity Attributes (Step 2)

- Project Schedule Network Diagram (Step 3)

- Resource Breakdown Structure (RBS) and Resource Calendars (Step 4)

- Activity Duration Estimates (Step 5)

Other key inputs impacting the overall project schedule requiring analysis include:

- Organizational Process Assets

- Enterprise Environmental Factors

- Risk Register

A Final input is project staff assignments. Project staff assignments specify which resources are assigned to each activity. These assignments impact the overall project schedule and are also subject to analysis.

Analyze Schedule Tools and Techniques

A number of tools and techniques are recommended to complete Step 6. We covered some tools in prior chapters. Others are new and require explanation.

- **Schedule Network Analysis:** Schedule network analysis is the tool generating the schedule model. This tool and technique is the use of any and all tools to create and execute a schedule model successfully. This includes selection of automated scheduling tools to support the project. All tools and techniques discussed below are part of the Project Scheduler's schedule network analysis toolbox.

- **Critical Chain Method:** Refer to Chapter 1. Critical Chain Method adds buffers in conjunction with various schedule activities to account for risk and other factors.

- **Leads and Lags:** Leads may be potentially available and lags may be necessitated as you analyze the schedule. Refer to Figure 3.5 for a review of leads and lags.

- **Critical Path Method (CPM):** CPM was introduced in Chapter 1. The CPM accomplishes three objectives. First, calculate the critical path. Second, conduct a "Forward Pass" to determine Early Start (ES) and Early Finish (EF) dates. Finally, conduct a Backward Pass to calculate the Late Start (LS) and Late Finish (LF) dates. Figure 3.13 provides an overview of CPM.

Figure 3.13 Critical Path Method Overview

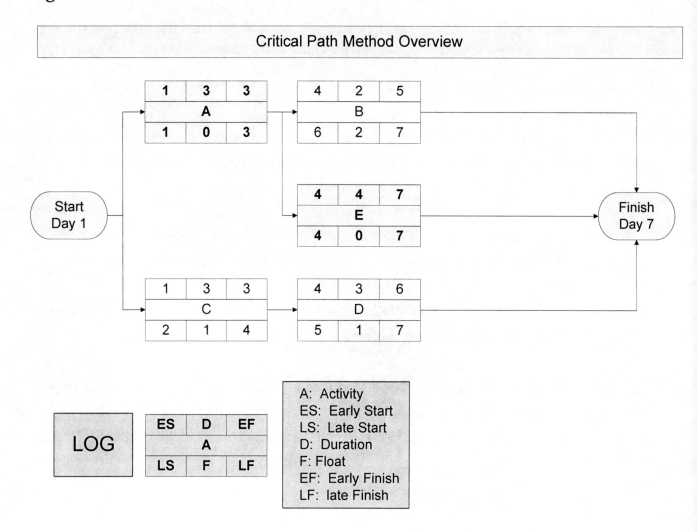

Critical Path Method Overview

LOG

ES	D	EF
	A	
LS	F	LF

A: Activity
ES: Early Start
LS: Late Start
D: Duration
F: Float
EF: Early Finish
LF: late Finish

Figure 3.13 Critical Path Method Overview Clarifying Notes and Steps

1. Calculate the Critical Path: There are three distinct paths in this network diagram. Durations (D) are provided. **The critical path is AE which is 7 days.**
   a. Path AB is 5 Days (3 + 2)
   b. Path AE is 7 Days (3 + 4)
   c. Path CD is 6 Days (3 + 3)

2. Perform a **"Forward Pass."** This calculates ES and EF for all activities.
   a. Begin with critical path (AE). Start (ES) at Day 1. Fill in EF based on duration.
   b. Example: Begin with Activity A. Work forward completing ES first, then EF. ES is Day 1. Duration is 3 days. EF is Day 3.
   c. Complete entire path. Activity E follows A. Begin on Day 4. Complete Day 7.
   d. Complete Forward Pass for all remaining paths beginning with path with most days. In this case path CD has 6 days. Do this path second. Finish with path AB.

3. Perform a **"Backward Pass."** This calculates LF and LS for all activities.
   a. Start with critical path again (AE). This time work backwards. Fill in the critical path of 7 days in the LF for Activity E. Count back based in the duration. Activity E has duration of 4 days. The LS is therefore day 4.
   b. Next move to Activity A. Subtract 1 day and fill in LF as day 3. Count down based on 3 day duration to fill in LS as day 1.
   c. Note float for path AE. It is zero (0). Float is calculated by comparing the difference between ES and LS, and difference between EF and LF. There is no difference.
   d. Next, choose the next longest path. Path CD is 6 days. Perform a Backwards Pass. Note there is a difference of 1 day between ES and LS and EF and LF. Path CD has one-day float. This is quite logical if you think about it. Path AE takes 7 days. Path CD takes 6 days. This is a difference of 1 day—hence the float.
   e. One activity is left, Activity B. Perform a Backwards Pass and you find Activity B has a float of 2 days.

- **Schedule Compression Techniques**: Schedule compression techniques are used to reduce or shorten project schedules without reducing project scope. There are two techniques—fast tracking and crashing. See Figure 3.14 after an overview of these two techniques.

  o *Fast Tracking:* Fast tracking eliminates dependencies for two activities planned to be completed sequentially. Fast tracking can only be accomplished for dependencies that are discretionary. Caution—fast tracking increases risk.

  o *Crashing:* Crashing involves using resources from non-critical path activities and applying them to critical path activities. Crashing often increases costs. Resources must stop what they are doing, orient themselves in the new environment, and restart prior activity work after the crashing activity is complete. In addition, crashing may pose a risk of creating a new critical path.

Figure 3.14 Schedule Compression Techniques

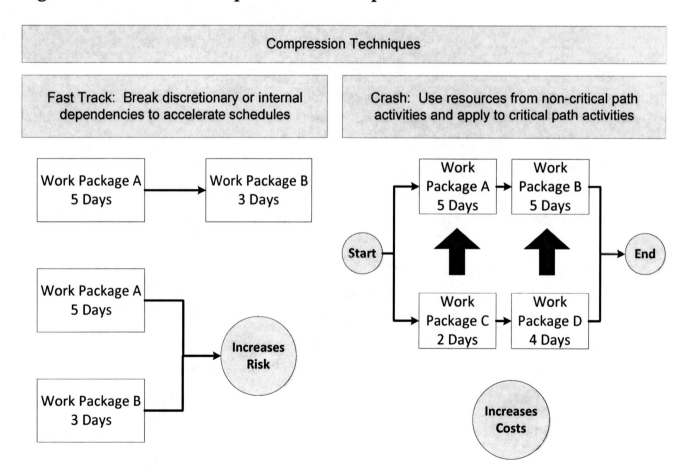

- **Resource Optimization Techniques**: Two Resource Optimization Techniques are used to analyze schedules to ensure they meet the needs of human resources assigned to project activities. Resource Optimization is used to adjust project resources to meet resource constraints, limited availability, or project changes. In addition, they are used when resources are over allocated and must be balanced out. Techniques include *Resource Leveling* and *Resource Smoothing*. Figure 3.15 shares these techniques. Here is an overview.

  o **Resource Leveling**: Adjust start and finish dates to balance demand for resources with supply. Often causes original critical path to change, usually to increase. Resource Leveling is balancing resources on critical path.

  o **Resource Smoothing**: Adjusts activities to ensure requirements for resources do not exceed certain pre-defined resource limits. Resource Smoothing does not impact critical path. Resources are adjusted or delayed within their free or total float. Resource Smoothing is balancing resources on the non-critical path.

Figure 3.15 Resource Optimization

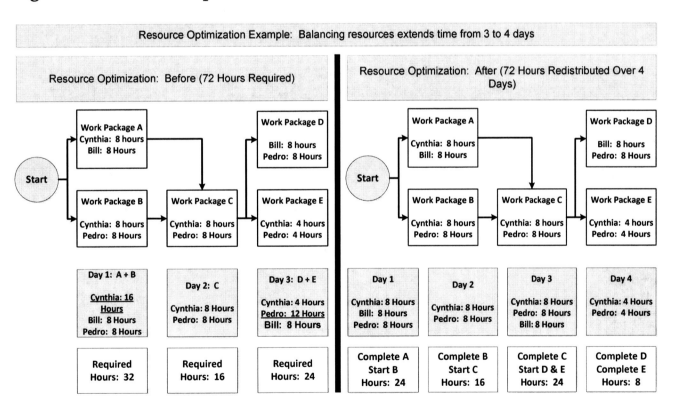

Figure 3.15 Resource Optimization Clarifying Notes

- Cynthia and Pedro are over allocated in this three-day scenario. The Project Scheduler needs to reduce daily working hours to 8 hours or less.

- The new optimized schedule reduces Cynthia and Pedro's workload to 8 hours or less. However, the schedule shifts from 3 to 4 days as a result.

- If this scenario was on the critical path, we would refer to this Resource Optimization activity as Resource Leveling. The critical path increases by 1 day.

- If this scenario was not on the critical path, we would refer to this Resource Optimization activity as Resource Smoothing. The critical path would not increase. However, you would lose 1 day of float.

- **Modeling Techniques:** Modeling techniques are tools and techniques to analyze a schedule. Here is a quick overview of two primary modeling techniques.

  o **What-If Scenario Analysis:** Process of evaluating scenarios to determine their effect on project objectives.

  o **Simulation:** Uses computer models, estimates of risk--expressed as probability distributions of both costs and durations, and typically uses a tool called *Monte Carlo*. Monte Carlo is highlighted in Figure 3.16.

    - Monte Carlo is an automated tool that provides probabilities of completing activity or project cost and schedule estimates.

    - Project Scheduler inputs the optimistic, most likely, and pessimistic estimates, along with activity dependencies into the tool to generate probabilities.

Figure 3.16 Monte Carlo

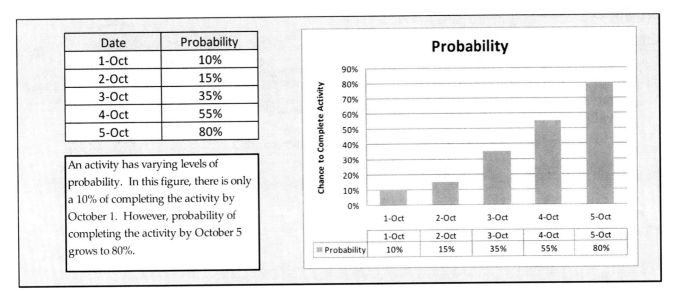

Date	Probability
1-Oct	10%
2-Oct	15%
3-Oct	35%
4-Oct	55%
5-Oct	80%

An activity has varying levels of probability. In this figure, there is only a 10% of completing the activity by October 1. However, probability of completing the activity by October 5 grows to 80%.

Analyze Schedule Output

The final output of this step is a proposed project schedule. As part of this output, a determination needs to be made on how to prepare presentations for sponsors and stakeholders to move forward with Step 7 in the Schedule Model Creation process — schedule approval.

There are three common methods used to prepare presentations. They include bar charts, milestone charts, and project schedule network diagrams. Figure 3.17 provides a brief overview of each.

Figure 3.17 Project Schedule Presentations

Milestone Chart

Code of Account/Activity Identifier	Jan	Feb	Mar	April	May	Jun
1.1 Improve Accounts Receivable Process	◇———————————————————▶◇					
1.1.1 Define Process	◇——▶◇					
1.1.2 Measure Process		◇——▶◇				
1.1.3 Analyze Process		◇———————▶◇				
1.1.4 Improve Process				◇———————▶◇		
1.1.5 Control Process					◇——▶◇	

Bar Chart

Code of Account/Activity Identifier	Jan	Feb	Mar	April	May	Jun
1.1 Improve Accounts Receivable Process	███████████					
1.1.1 Define Process	████					
1.1.2 Measure Process		████▢				
1.1.3 Analyze Process		████▢				
1.1.4 Improve Process				▢▢▢		
1.1.5 Control Process					▢▢	

Data Date

Note: Bar Charts are frequently used in management presentations

Project Network Diagram

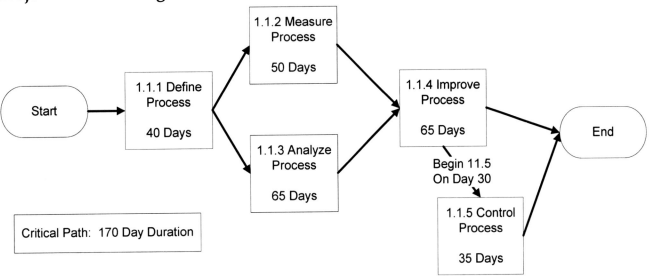

Start → 1.1.1 Define Process 40 Days → 1.1.2 Measure Process 50 Days → 1.1.4 Improve Process 65 Days → End

1.1.3 Analyze Process 65 Days → 1.1.4 Improve Process

Begin 11.5 On Day 30

1.1.5 Control Process 35 Days → End

Critical Path: 170 Day Duration

Approve and Baseline the Schedule

There are two final steps in the Schedule Creation process. Figure 3.18 is provided for reference. *Approve the Schedule* by presenting the proposed schedule to the Project Sponsor. Then present the proposed schedule to Stakeholders for acceptance. You *Baseline the Schedule* once the schedule is approved and accepted.

Figure 3.18 Schedule Model Creation Excerpt #6

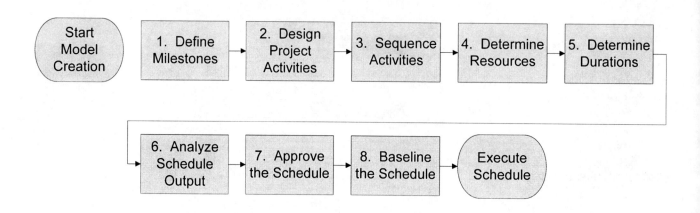

Approval of the project schedule and subsequent creation of the Schedule Baseline is a step-by-step process as well. Figure 3.19 provides an overview.

Figure 3.19 Project Schedule Baseline Development Process

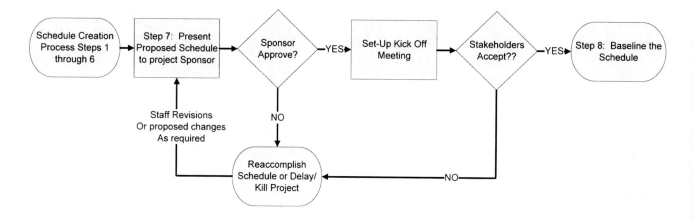

Notes:

- Project manager presents the proposed project schedule to a Project Sponsor. Project Sponsor either approves schedule, or requests reaccomplishment of the schedule. In some cases, a project may be killed due to the schedule unable to support project objectives. A key role of a project manager is to recommend good projects move forward, and poor projects get killed. Not every project plan should be implemented.

- The project manager or Project Scheduler next gains stakeholder acceptance of the schedule once the Sponsor approves the proposed schedule. A project *Kick-Off Meeting* is set up to gain required stakeholder acceptance. You may gain acceptance, or stakeholders may provide rationale to change the schedule or even kill the project. If this occurs, share stakeholder inputs with the Project Sponsor to determine next steps.

- Once stakeholders accept the proposed schedule, the *Schedule Baseline* is established. Use the Baseline Schedule to measure performance, determine variances, determine impact of changes, and adjust schedule components as needed. The Baseline Schedule can only be changed through the formal Integrated Change Control process and serves as the basis for successful project completion. The Schedule Baseline serves as the guide to project Execution.

Schedule Planning and Development: Additional Topics

Here are a few additional topics in the Schedule Planning and Development domain.

- **Critical Path versus Critical Activities:** *Critical Activities* are activities vital to success of the project. Critical activities normally are the most complex activities, or those with high risk. *Critical Path* is defined as the path of longest duration on a Project Network Diagram. All activities on Critical Path are considered critical activities because of the risk of missing a scheduled completion that could lengthen the project schedule.

- **Free Float versus Total Float:** *Free Float* is defined as the amount of time an activity's Early Finish Date may be delayed without impacting a successor activity Early Start Date. Free float indicates how a lack of progress impacts immediate successors. *Total Float* is the amount of time an activity Early Start or Early Finish Date may be delayed without impacting the Late Finish Date of the entire project or violating a schedule model constraint date. Total float changes indicate a threat to complete the project on time as planned.

- **Negative Float:** *Negative float* occurs when an activity start date is later than the forecast finish date. For example, Activity A may now be scheduled to begin on Day 15 due to schedule delays. The original completion forecast was Day 13. Activity A has a negative float of -2. Address negative float by changing schedule logic, crashing, fast tracking, or gaining Sponsor approval to change the schedule.

- **Level of Effort (LOE) Activities**: Some project activities are designated to support other work activities or the entire project. Some examples could be accounting, customer liaison, or security, etc. Duration is based on the duration of all activities it supports. For example, security for the site begins on Day 1 and spans all activities until project end. *LOE* activities usually use SS or FF relationships. LOE activities are often referred to as a *Hammock Activity*. It may also be referred to as a *Summary Activity*. Figure 3.20 shows an LOE, or Hammock/Summary, activity.

Figure 3.20 LOE Activity

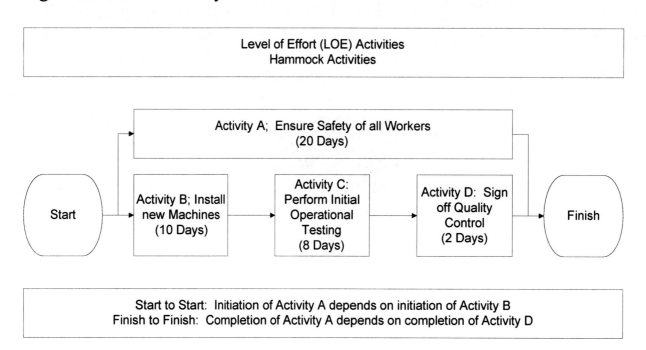

- **Integrated Master Plan (IMP) and the Integrated Master Schedule (IMS):** These are important program management tools providing assistance in the planning and scheduling of work efforts in large and complex materiel acquisitions

- **Performance Measurement Baseline:** *Performance Measurement Baseline (PMB) is the* approved plan for accomplishing all project work to include scope, cost, and schedule. May additionally incorporate both technical and quality parameters as well.

- **Activity Network Diagram (AND):** Diagram of project activities showing the most realistic path and schedule for project completion. Graphically shows tasks, dependencies, and critical activities.

Chapter 3 Summary

This chapter discussed Domain 2 of the PMI-SP Certification Exam. Schedule Planning and Development is a time-consuming process that follows a step-by-step Schedule Model Creation Process.

We covered a number of concepts, definitions, and additional applications necessary to effectively plan and develop a schedule that meets the needs of the project. Remember, this domain addressed 31% of all questions on the PMI-SP Certification Exam.

Challenge yourself to complete Activity 3B. Responses are listed in Appendix A.

Activity 3B: Schedule Model Creation Steps 5 - 8

Directions: Match the scenario or definition to the potential responses provided.

Schedule Planning and Development (Steps 5 - 8)	Response
1. Involves using resources from non-critical path activities and applying them to critical path activities. Often increases costs	
2. Uses WBS as a guide. Each Work Package is individually estimated for time durations and costs. Best used for complex and ambiguous projects where there are many unknowns	
3. Techniques used to adjust project resources to meet resource constraints, limited availability, or project changes	
4. Delays the start of the successor activity even though the predecessor activity may be complete	
5. Weighted estimation model based on norms that state the Optimistic and Pessimistic results occur approximately one out of every six times, and the Most Likely result occurs approximately four out of six times	
6. Most frequently used schedule presentation type for management presentations	
7. Reserves that address times when project risks cannot be identified until planning progresses, or even project execution begins	
8. Meeting that presents a proposed project schedule to stakeholders for review and acceptance. Occurs after Sponsor approval	
9. Reserves that address risks identified on the Risk Register. Addresses known unknowns	
10. Project activities are designated to support other work activities or the entire project. Often referred to as "Hammock Activities"	
11. Tool that generates the schedule model. This tool and technique is the use of any and all tools to create and execute a schedule model successfully	
12. Technique uses actual durations of previous, similarly scheduled activities or entire projects as a basis for time estimates. Most reliable when past projects are similar in fact and not just appearance	
13. Adjust start and finish dates to balance demand for resources with supply. Often causes the original critical path to change, usually to increase	

14. Eliminates dependencies for two activities planned to be completed sequentially. Can only be accomplished for dependencies that are not mandatory	
15. Uses computer models, estimates of risk--expressed as probability distributions of both costs and durations, and typically uses a tool called Monte Carlo	
16. Estimation uses three distinct estimates. Determine an Optimistic estimate, Most-Likely Estimate, and Pessimistic Estimate and use mathematical models to determine the best estimate	
17. Adjusts activities to ensure requirements for resources do not exceed certain pre-defined resource limits. Does not impact critical path. Resources are adjusted or delayed within their free or total float	
18. Initial Project Network Diagram does not include time durations. It simply shows the logical flow of all activities based on dependency determinations	
19. Sums three estimates and uses the average to determine the final estimate. Also called a *Triangular Distribution*	
20. Technique quantitatively multiplies the quantity of work to be performed × the productivity rate. Uses regression analysis and learning curve techniques	

Activity 3B: Choose from the following:

A. Lag

B. Analogous, Top Down, Expert Estimating

C. Pure Logic Diagram

D. Parametric Estimating

E. Crashing

F. Resource Optimization Techniques

G. PERT

H. Bottom Up Estimating

I. Management Reserves

J. Three-Point Averaging Method

K. Level of Effort (LOE) Activity

L. Three-Point Estimating

M. Simulation

N. Resource Leveling

O. Contingency Reserves

P. Bar Chart

Q. Resource Smoothing

R. Schedule Network Analysis

S. Kick-Off Meeting

T. Fast Tracking

Peter's Real World Perspective #1

One of the biggest mistakes is to commit to a project finish date without developing a realistic project schedule. *"We don't have time to develop a real project schedule,"* or *"We don't know the full project scope, so we will schedule as much as we can."* Imagine the risk of committing to a date and not knowing how to get there, or exactly what you need to deliver!

Project teams delude themselves into thinking that they will figure it out, or that a miracle will save them. When was the last time you witnessed a miracle?

The project team, and the project manager in particular, must be bold, tough, and courageous. They must again, *Go Slow Now to Go Fast Later* – do the planning, the scheduling necessary to reduce schedule risk, the uncertainty in the schedule to an acceptable level. And, regardless of the level of risk in the schedule, the project manager must communicate the risk to the customer, the sponsor, and other key stakeholders external to the core project team. These stakeholders must know and understand that there is schedule risk and that the project team will do its best to manage this risk so that the project meets it's time commitments.

In later chapters we cover risk, how to communicate risk, and how to manage stakeholder expectations. More on those subjects then!

Chapter 4: Schedule Monitoring and Controlling

We now turn attention to Domain 3 of the PMI-SP Certification Exam. The Schedule Monitoring and Controlling domain is 35% of the examination. The focus of this domain is monitoring schedule progress, performing schedule analysis, and ensuring change is managed properly.

Control Schedule

The Time Management Chapter of the *PMBOK* defines schedule control basics in the Control Schedule process. A key goal of this process is providing a means to recognize when schedule variances occur, manage and control schedule related risks, and take preventative or corrective actions necessary to overcome variances and keep the project schedule on-track.

Control Schedule Inputs

- **Project Management Plan (Schedule Baseline):** Contains the Schedule Baseline, which is the standard all performance is compared against. In addition, the Schedule Management Plan provides guidance on managing change.

- **Work Performance Data (Schedule Data):** The Project Scheduler receives numerous project related data from key stakeholders to analyze and take action upon as necessary. The key is extracting applicable schedule data. This data is produced during the Executing Process Group and used to adequately monitor and control the project schedule. The Project Scheduler analyzes *Work Performance Data* and creates *Work Performance Information*. Work Performance Data is raw data providing various pieces of information. Work Performance Information takes data and formats it to provide useable information regarding schedule performance to be consumed and used by stakeholders. Work Performance Information is a key input to the project *Work Performance Report*.

- **Project Calendars:** This calendar is initially assigned to define working and non-working times for schedule activities and resources. Typically defines holidays, weekend work schedules, working hours, etc. There may be single or multiple calendars. A specific project calendar allows the Project Scheduler to monitor and control planned availability of resources for the project. Multiple calendars allow the Project Scheduler to determine if there are resource conflicts with other projects. Project calendars are adjusted as project schedule needs change.

- **Organizational Process Assets:** Policies, procedures, and preferred methodology impact the monitor and control function. In addition, most organizations have pre-determined status reporting tools and guidelines to follow.

Control Schedule Tools and Techniques

- **Performance Reviews:** The Project Scheduler reviews and reports schedule performance. Some options:

  - **Trend Analysis:** Most schedule issues don't occur without warning. Trend analysis dictates reviewing planned versus actual performance over time to determine if the schedule is trending well or poorly. Solid trend analysis allows you to identify proactively address issues. For example, your project may be two weeks behind schedule. However, if the trend over the past month went from four weeks behind to two weeks behind, it shows corrective measures taken are working.

  - **Critical Path Method (CPM):** Updating the Project Network Diagram as activities are started and/or completed is a great way to determine whether schedule is on track. If critical path has seven activities, and if you are behind by three days after completion of Activity 3, you can potentially fast track or crash to try to get the schedule back on track.

  - **Critical Chain Method:** Critical Chain Method uses buffers to address risk. Reviewing how buffers worked is critical. There may be some buffers you didn't need which is good news. Other buffers may have underestimated the risk. This scenario is a great reason to perform *Lessons Learned* and share findings with other project managers so they can take advantage of the learnings you gather over the course of a project. The primary reason to conduct Lessons Learned is helping future project managers succeed.

o **Earned Value Management (EVM):** An important section of this chapter is devoted to EVM. This is a preferred means of tracking schedule status quantitatively and is a huge point of interest on the certification test. Don't be surprised to see between five to 15 questions on EVM.

o **Other Tools and Techniques:** You will leverage many techniques discussed in previous chapters as you monitor and control project schedule. These may include leads and lags, Compression Techniques as fast-tracking and crashing, Resource Optimization techniques as Resource Leveling and Resource Smoothing, and Modeling Techniques as What-If Analysis and Simulation using Monte Carlo.

Control Schedule Outputs

- **Schedule Forecasts:** Stakeholders need to know project status. Oftentimes, schedule is the number one priority. The Project Scheduler role generally shares schedule status in Work Performance Reports. Primary concerns are where the schedule is today, and how the schedule is tracking toward successful completion. EVM provides data to share that enables forecasting.

- **Manage Change:** The Project Scheduler must be aware of all planned and unplanned project changes potentially impacting schedule success. Ensure all changes are processed through Integrated Change Control.

- **Updates:** Update the Project Management Plan and other documentation throughout the project. Project change impacts multiple aspects of the schedule model. This includes affected Organizational Process Assets as well. Changes happen.

Schedule Monitoring and Controlling: Key Responsibilities

There are many Project Scheduler responsibilities. Here is an overview of a few that can make or break a project.

- **Interact with Activity Owners:** Each WBS activity should have an owner. The Project Scheduler ensures each activity has a capable owner assigned, and interfaces with this owner on a consistent basis to collect activity status, address issues, facilitate meetings or inspections, share changes, and provide updates.

- **Collect Resource Information:** The Project Scheduler reviews Work Performance Data to include reports, timesheets, meeting minutes, inspection reports, the RBS, etc., to analyze and report resource utilization and availability. Don't assume your initial plan will remain intact throughout the project. Some organizations may establish *Resource Groups*. These groups may be organized by skill sets, organizational assignments, work categorization or more. The Project Scheduler needs to understand how Resource Groups are organized, who controls each group, and how each group potentially impacts the resources required to successfully achieve schedule goals. Conditions impacting resources are in a constant state of flux. The Project Scheduler must stay current and address issues as they develop.

- **Perform Audits:** *Quality Audits* ensure project standards are followed and prevent potential problems from occurring. Quality Audits are accomplished as part of the Quality Assurance process during the Executing Process Group. The Project Scheduler performs periodic quality audits to ensure in-house and contractor activities are occurring as planned, and identify any preventative changes or issues needing to be addressed.

- **Provide Options:** There are times when the Schedule Baseline is in jeopardy of completion. The Project Scheduler identifies and analyzes issues, and proposes options to get the schedule back on track. Some options discussed previously include Resource Optimization Techniques, Compression Techniques, What-If Scenario Analysis, Monte Carlo analysis, etc.

- **Forensic Schedule Analysis:** *Forensic Schedule Analysis* is the study of event interaction using CPM or other popular scheduling tools to understand why deviations from the Schedule Baseline occurred. Forensic Schedule Analysis may be used for legal proceedings, and is performed retrospectively with the goal of identifying true causes and impacts of schedule delays. The Project Scheduler may perform this type of analysis if circumstances dictate.

- **Risk Management:** The project Risk Register lists risks potentially impacting a project. The Project Scheduler needs to understand the impact of risk on all schedule components, and mitigate effects of negative risk by implementing change control to change the overall Performance Management Baseline. Three-Point averaging or PERT estimation is a great way to accommodate risk into the project schedule.

- **Externalities:** The Project Scheduler needs to understand industry standards, external regulations and organizational guidelines that may constrain or create external dependencies impacting the project schedule. Knowledge of industry best practices may allow opportunities to accelerate the schedule.

Earned Value Management

Earned Value Management (EVM) is an industry standard to measure planned versus actual schedule and cost performance. It provides a status snapshot of schedule and cost status, shows trends, and is essential for forecasting. This section defines EVM, shares examples, and challenges you with an EVM activity.

Figure 4.1 provides an overview of key EVM terminology. Understand terms and acronyms used throughout this section.

Figure 4.1 EVM Terminology

Term	Acronym	Definition
Planned Value	PV	Estimated value of work planned to be accomplished at a given time
Earned Value	EV	Estimated value of work already accomplished
Actual Costs	AC	Actual cost of work already accomplished
Budget at Completion	BAC	Amount budgeted for entire project

EVM Scenario A

Here is a scenario showing how to extract EVM cost data:

You are managing the ABC project, and it is 50% complete. Your total BAC is $100,000. You planned to be 60% complete at this point in the project. To date, you have actually spent $65,000 on the project.

Review information provided to calculate EV, AC, and PV values. This allows you to perform EVM calculations.

- BAC is $100,000. Assume this is the value of the project.

- You completed 50% of a $100,000 project. Your EV reflects the value of work completed. This is calculated as 50% times $100,000, or $50,000.

- AC reflects actual money spent. In this scenario, AC is given as $65,000. You spent $65,000 to attain $50,000 in EV. You are over budget!

- You planned to be 60% complete at this point in the project. The PV is calculated as 60% times $100,000, or $60,000.

Notes: Clarification regarding EVM and the test:

- In the real world, some projects attain higher EV levels than BAC. However, for test purposes, 100% of EV will always equal the BAC. In the scenario above, a 100% project completion attains EV of $100,000. If you only completed 20%, then the EV is calculated as 20% times $100,000 = $20,000.

- Always assume PV is linear. In our scenario, PV is 60%. This means you planned to achieve 60% times BAC of $100,000, or $60,000.

- Advanced EVM models consider non-linear returns and EV values greater than BAC. However, you will not encounter these scenarios on the certification test.

Activity 4A: EVM Practice Scenarios

Scenario 1: Your project delivered 60% of all required deliverables. You planned to be 70% complete with the entire project at this time. You spent $50,000 of your total $100,000 BAC allocation.

Calculate EV, PV, and AC into dollar amounts.

EV	
PV	
AC	

Scenario 2: A six month project has a PV of $40,000 every two months. What is the BAC for this project?

BAC	

It is now time to expand understanding of EVM. Figure 4.2 provides additional EVM definitions.

Figure 4.2 Additional EVM Terminology

Term	Acronym	Definition
Schedule Variance	SV	Measure of schedule performance. Negative SV means project is behind schedule. Positive SV means project is ahead of schedule.
Cost Variance	CV	Measure of cost performance. Negative CV means project is over budget. Positive CV means project is under budget.

Schedule Performance Index	SPI	Measure of schedule performance. SPI < 1 means project is behind schedule. SPI > 1 means project is ahead of schedule.
Cost Performance Index	CPI	Measure of cost performance. CPI < 1 means project is over budget. CPI > 1 means project is ahead on budget.
Estimate at Completion	EAC	Current estimate of how much the project will cost at completion based on status to date.
Estimate to Complete	ETC	From this point forward, how much more the project expected to cost.
Variance at Completion	VAC	At end of the project, how much over or under budget is the project.
To Complete Performance Index	TCPI	Level of effort required to complete a project based on BAC or EAC.

EVM Scenario A Expanded

Scenario A presented a problem and asked you to calculate the EV, PV, and AC. We can use this scenario to expand upon our project analysis calculating additional performance measures.

Scenario A: Your project is 60% complete. You planned to be 70% complete at this time. You spent $50,000 of your $100,000 BAC. (EV, PV, and AC are shown below.) Figure 4.3 provides formulas and solutions for performance metrics defined in Figure 4.2.

- EV = 60% × $100,000 = $60,000

- PV = 70% × $100,000 = $70,000

- **AC = $50,000**

Figure 4.3 Base EVM Calculations

Base EVM Calculations	Answer	Interpretation
SV = EV - PV	$60,000 – $70,000 = -$10,000	You planned to complete $70,000 of work. You completed $60,000. You are behind by $10,000 of work.
CV = EV - AC	$60,000 - $50,000 = $10,000	You completed $60,000 of work. You only paid $50,000. You are ahead on budget by $10,000.
SPI = EV/PV	$60,000/$70,000 = .86	The schedule is progressing at 86% of the plan. You are behind schedule.
CPI = EV/AC	$60,000/$50,000 = 1.2	You are realizing $1.20 in value for every $1.00 you spend. You are ahead on budget.
EAC = BAC/CPI	$100,000/1.2 = $83,333	If you continue to realize $1.20 for each $1.00 you spend, total project cost will be $83,333.
ETC = EAC - AC	$83,333 - $50,000 = $33,333	You spent $50,000. If the project only costs $83,333, you need an additional $33,333 to complete.
VAC = BAC - EAC	$100,000 - $83,333 = $16,667	Your BAC is $100,000. The EAC is only $83,333. If the project comes in under budget, you save $16,667.
TCPI for BAC Value of Work Remaining/ Value of Budget Remaining	$\dfrac{\$40,000 \; (BAC - EV)}{\$50,000 \; (BAC - AC)}$ Answer = 0.8	You are ahead on budget. If you are willing to finish the project and spend the entire BAC, you can reduce workload. If people are working 8 hours a day, multiply 8 times the TCPI to determine the new work schedule. In this scenario, that is 8 × 0.8 = 6.4 hours. **Note:** This break for workers allows you to still complete the project at BAC. However, you are behind schedule. Reduction of work hours will make matters worse.

TCPI for EAC Value of Work Remaining/ETC	$40,000 (BAC – EV) $33,333 (ETC) Answer = 1.20	The ETC of $33,333 considers this project is ahead of budget. The TCPI rating of 1.2 states you need to continue to get 1.2 hours of productivity for every one hour worked. You are achieving that now. However, you could guarantee the project only costs $83,333 (EAC) by increasing work hours. In this scenario, that would work out as 8 × 1.2 = 9.6 hours each day. The workers won't be happy, but you'll be guaranteed to achieve an under budget project.

In this scenario, you are currently ahead on budget, but behind on schedule. The goal of every project is to finish on-time, within budget, and provide scope promised in the Project Management Plan. Figure 4.4 provides four scenarios and strategies to address various conditions. Apply guidance in this table.

Figure 4.4 EVM Strategy

Project Status	Strategy—Action to Take
SPI is > 1.0. CPI is < 1.0	Value Analysis
SPI is < 1.0. CPI is > 1.0	Crash
SPI is < 1.0. CPI is < 1.0	Fast Track & Value Analysis
SPI is > 1.0. CPI is > 1.0	Find Out Why and Analyze

Notes:

- **Value Analysis:** Value analysis is defined as finding a cheaper way to accomplish project activities. Value analysis is always an option when over budget.

- **Crashing:** Crashing is only an option when you are under budget. In the Figure 4.3 scenario, crashing is the preferred strategy to leverage additional budget you have to get the schedule back on track.

- **Fast Tracking:** Fast tracking adds risk. Only use fast tracking when you lack additional resources and budget to crash.

There are various question types you may encounter using EVM. Some questions require calculations, while others may be simple concept based word problems to solve. There are times when algebra is required. Figure 4.5 shows variations of the base EVM formulas.

Figure 4.5 EVM Formula Variations

Base EVM Calculations	Variation 1	Variation 2
CV = EV - AC	AC = EV - CV	EV = CV + AC
SV = EV - PV	PV = EV - SV	EV = SV + PV
CPI = EV/AC	AC = EV/CPI	EV = CPI × AC
SPI = EV/PV	PV = EV/SPI	EV = SPI × PV

Example 1: Your project CV is -$300. Your AC is $1,000. What is the EV?

- **Solution:** EV = CV + AC (-$300 + $1,000 = $700)

Example 2: Your project SPI is 0.8. Your EV is $1,000. What is the PV?

- **Solution:** PV = EV/SPI ($1,000/0.8 = $1,250)

EVM Summary

Anticipate numerous EVM questions on the certification test. The Schedule Monitoring and Control Domain include 35% of all PMI-SP Certification Exam questions. EVM questions account for a large number. Activity 4B poses additional EVM scenarios. Use these scenarios to prepare for EVM questions.

Activity 4B: EVM Practice Scenarios

1. You planned to complete 60% of a $50,000 project by this time. You completed 70% of the project. Actual Cost to this point are $35,000. Calculate SV, CV, SPI, CPI, and EAC.

2. SV is $200 and CV $ -200. Your EV is $3,000. Calculate PV and AC.

3. CPI is .8. AC is $2,500. Calculate EV.

4. SPI is .91. EV is $2,000. Calculate PV. Round to nearest hundred dollars.

5. EV is $1,000. AC is $900 and PV is $950. Calculate CPI and SPI.

6. EV is $20,000. AC is $30,000 and PV is $25,000. Calculate TCPI for this this project to achieve a BAC goal of $50,000.

Answers:

1.	
2.	
3.	
4.	
5.	
6.	

Progress Reporting

Progress Reporting: It is difficult and generally not practical to request actual percentages of work complete. However, calculating percentage complete is critical to determining project EV. There are three methods of calculating *Activity Duration Percent Complete* that may appear on the certification test. Figure 4.6 shows an example of various progress reporting methods.

1. **50/50 Rule:** Activity is considered 50% complete when it begins. Credit the last 50% when completed.

2. **20/80 Rule:** Activity is considered 20% complete when it begins. Credit the last 80% when completed.

3. **0/100 Rule:** Activity gets zero partial credit. It is deemed 100% complete when closed out.

Figure 4.6 Progress Reporting Scenario

Work Package	Status	50/50	20/80	0/100
A	Complete	100	100	100
B	Complete	100	100	100
C	Started	50	20	
D	Started	50	20	
E				
% Complete		300/500 = 60%	240/500 = 48%	200/500 = 40%

Figure 4.6 Explanation: Project has five Work Packages: A, B, C, D, and E.

- **Work Package Status:** Work Packages A and B are complete. Work Packages C and D are started but not complete. Work Package E has not started.

- **50/50:** Using 50/50 progress reporting, all completed Work Packages are awarded 100 points. You award 50 points when you start a Work Package. You receive 0 points when a Work Package is not started. Total score for the project is 300 points. To determine percent complete or EV, divide total project score by total points available. In this scenario there are 5 Work Packages times 100 points each when complete for a total of 500 points. The math: 300/500 = 60% complete.

- **20/80:** Using 20/80 progress reporting, completed Work Packages are awarded 100 points. Award 20 points when starting a Work Package. You receive 0 points when a Work Package is not started. Total score for the project is 240 points. Use the same calculation as the 50/50 method. The math: 240/500 = 48% complete.

- **0/100:** Using 0/100 progress reporting, all completed Work Packages are awarded 100 points. You receive 0 points when you start a Work Package. Total score for this project is 200 points. Use the same calculation method used for the 50/50 method. The math: 200/500 = 40% complete.

Note: Define progress reporting methods in the Schedule Management Plan.

Network Diagram Analysis

A key objective of the Schedule Monitoring and Controlling domain is to perform schedule analysis. Figure 4.7 provides a Project Network Diagram to analyze and discuss.

Figure 4.7 Sample Project Network Diagram

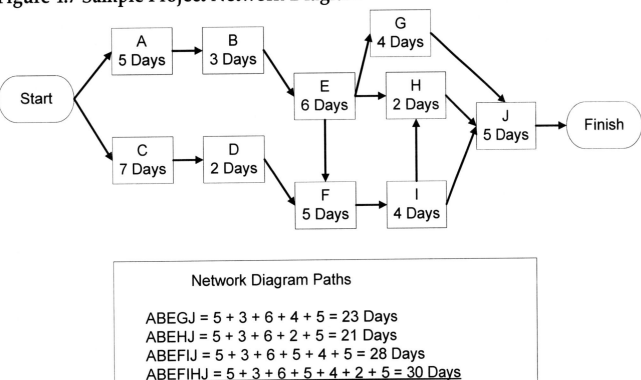

Network Diagram Paths

ABEGJ = 5 + 3 + 6 + 4 + 5 = 23 Days
ABEHJ = 5 + 3 + 6 + 2 + 5 = 21 Days
ABEFIJ = 5 + 3 + 6 + 5 + 4 + 5 = 28 Days
ABEFIHJ = 5 + 3 + 6 + 5 + 4 + 2 + 5 = 30 Days
CDFIJ = 7 + 2 + 5 + 4 + 5 = 23 Days
CDFIHJ = 7 + 2 + 5 + 4 + 2 + 5 = 25 Days

Notes:

- **Critical Path:** There are six possible paths from start to finish. *Critical path* is the path of longest duration. In this example, path ABEFIHJ is 30 Days. This is critical path. Critical path is also the amount of time it takes to finish the project. This project will take 30 days to complete. If critical path changes, amount of time to complete the project also changes.

- **Float:** There are three activities not on critical path with *float*. Those activities are C, D, and G. Crashing can be accomplished using resources from these three activities. For example, Activity B is in jeopardy of being delayed which would impact critical path. You may use resources from any activity with float but beware. Crashing may cost you additional budget due to additional time required to move resources from activity to activity, orient personnel resources to the new environment, and gain inertia lost by stopping and starting diverse tasks. Here is an overview of float each activity provides:

- o **Activity C:** Activity C is part of two paths. Path CDFIJ requires 23 days to complete and path CDFIHJ requires 25 days to complete. To calculate float, subtract the longest path Activity C is a part of from the critical path. The result is $30 - 25 = 5$ days.

- o **Activity D:** Activity D is part of the same two paths as Activity C. Float is 5 days.

- o **Activity G:** Activity G is on one path ABEGJ. This path has duration of 23 days. The float is $30 - 23 = 7$ days.

- **Duration Changes and Additions:** Here are potential duration changes/additions and their effect:

  - o **Near Critical Path:** Activity G incurs a risk that increases duration from 4 days to 10 days. That increases the time to complete path ABEGJ from 23 to 29 days. Path ABEGJ is now **"Near Critical Path."** This means any additional change may create two critical paths, or potentially ABEGJ may become the new critical path.

  - o **Addition:** A change adds new Activity K. Activity K has 6 day duration. Activity K occurs after Activity I and before Activity J. A new path is created. New path CDFIKJ replaces path CDFIJ. The new duration is $7 + 2 + 5 + 4 + 6 + 5 = 29$ Days. Critical path remains 30 days. However, a near critical path condition is created.

Activity 4C: Network Diagram Analysis Activity

Review the Project Network Diagram and answer questions below. Responses are in Appendix A.

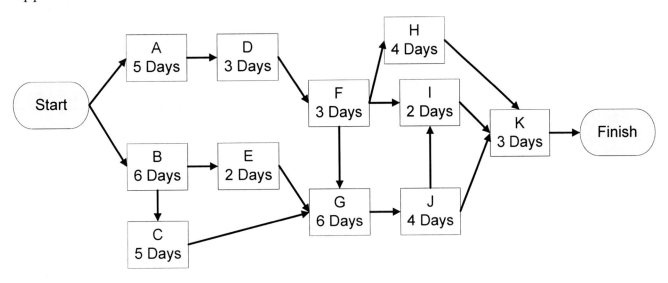

What is critical path?	
Which activities have float?	
A new Activity L is added between Activity J and K. Activity L is 3 Days. Impact?	
After Activity L is added, what is "Near Critical Path"?	
After Activity L is added, how much float does Activity I have if any?	

Managing Project Change

Projects seldom occur exactly as planned. Therefore, a system of change control is necessary. This system is referred to as *Integrated Change Control*. Schedule change requests occur. The Project Scheduler controls change as follows:

- **Develop the Process:** Develop an Integrated Change Control process to address how schedule changes are managed. This process is normally part of an overall project change process addressing all change types.

- **Share the Process:** The Integrated Change Control process is input into the project Communications Management Plan. The process includes instructions on how to submit changes, a change form, and change log available for review by all stakeholders.

- **Evangelize the Process:** Share the process with all stakeholders and encourage its use. Ask the project Sponsor to support the process and encourage stakeholders to use it. Reward those who use the process—maybe only a simple thank you—and address those who do not follow the process.

The *PMBOK* addresses Integrated Change Control. Here are highlights:

Integrated Change Control Inputs

- **Project Management Plan:** Contains the approved and accepted Schedule Baseline. The Project Scheduler compares proposed changes against the Schedule Baseline to determine impact. Some changes may occur that are not formally presented. The Project Scheduler needs to be alert to these changes and deal with them using the formal change process.

- **Work Performance Reports:** The Project Scheduler needs to review Work Performance Reports and perform *variance analysis*. Compare planned versus actual project results, look for variations, and address them.

- **Change Requests:** There are four types of changes a Project Scheduler must be aware of. Three are generally internal and a fourth is generally external.

  o **Preventative:** Preventative changes are usually recommended by the team and address potential problems. Preventative changes are often identified during Quality Assurance and propose changes to the Project Management Plan, or some aspect of how the project is being executed. Review changes for potential schedule impact.

o **Corrective:** Corrective changes are necessitated by deliverables not meeting plan specifications. Corrective Changes are often identified during Quality Control and propose ways to correct actual issues preventing successful completion of deliverables. Review changes for potential schedule impact.

o **Defect Repair:** There are times when a single deliverable is faulty and needs repair. Defect repair changes are normally identified during Quality Control. Time to correct a defect repair may impact the overall project schedule.

o **Stakeholder Driven:** Any stakeholder may request a change. Normally this change category requires the greatest level of analysis and poses the biggest challenge to the Schedule Baseline. The Project Scheduler needs to be involved in evaluation of stakeholder driven changes.

Integrated Change Control Tools and Techniques

- **Meetings:** Meetings are a common way to evaluate and process change requests.

- **Tools:** Change control tools are manual or automated methods used to manage the Integrated Change Control process. They vary by project.

Integrated Change Control Outputs

- **Change Decisions:** Decisions to approve, reject, defer, or reevaluate changes are key Integrated Change Control outputs. These decisions impact the project schedule.

- **Change Log:** Each project requires a change log documenting change requests and status. This change log is available for review by all stakeholders.

- **Project Management Plan Updates:** It is imperative the Project Management Plan be updated whenever a change occurs. The Project Team delivers what is in the plan. The only way to legally change the Schedule Baseline is through the Integrated Change Control process. All approved changes flow back to the Executing team.

There are a number of key concepts to understand in this section. Here is a brief synopsis:

- The project manager manages the change process. The project manager is responsible for evaluating changes, and prioritizing approved changes to implement first.

- All approved changes are incorporated into the project baseline. Process changes promptly.

- *The #1 goal* of change management is to *influence factors* that cause change. Accomplish this by having a transparent and well-communicated change control system.

- Project managers ensure all changes are reviewed and EITHER approved or denied/rejected by a defined authority. Authors may be the project management team, sponsor or an external organization.

- The complete impact of changes across the entire project should be reviewed and documented.

- *Changes may be requested by any stakeholder involved in the project.* Both written and verbal changes must be reviewed. Written submissions are encouraged.

- The project manager defines the process to manage changes. *(Normally included in Communications Management Plan)*

The Integrated Change Control Management Process

PMI recommends a four-step process.

1. **Log and Evaluate the Impact of the Requested Change.** The project manager determines how changes, if approved, impact the *triple constraints: time, cost, and scope.* Additional constraints must also be considered.

   - **Note 1:** If the project manager believes the change has no value, they still must evaluate the impact.

   - **Note 2:** If a change occurs you were not aware of, start here. All changes, both planned and unplanned must be logged and evaluated.

2. **Determine Options to Implement the Change**. If a change is approved, how can it be implemented? Two common "Compression Techniques" discussed previously include:

- **Fast Tracking:** Option allows two activities or Work Packages previously planned for sequential accomplishment to begin simultaneously. This option adds risk.

- **Crashing:** This option adds resources to a given Work Package to expedite completion. Resources are generally pulled from other Work Packages, and costs may increase.

3. **Coordinate with the Approval Authority:** Coordinate changes through the approval level defined in the Project Management Plan. There may be times when a change is rejected.

- A *Change Control Board, or CCB,* is an external group that reviews and approves/disapproves changes. Form a CCB if the project is large, requires high-levels of technical expertise, or has a high-degree of competing stakeholder interests. The project manager is a mandatory participant.

- You may need to include a review with the customer as a pre- or post-step based on sponsorship guidance.

4. **Process the Change and Gain Buy-In:** Formally act upon the approval or rejection. Try to gain the buy-in of stakeholders. Communicate results and update the Project Baseline as required.

Schedule Monitoring and Controlling: Additional Topics

Additional topics to be aware of in the Schedule Monitoring and Controlling domain:

- **Quality Management Plan Link:** The Quality Management Plan identifies critical Quality Assurance and Quality Control metrics essential to project success. Many metrics are directly impacted by schedule performance. Know schedule related metrics and compare planned versus actual performance as a part of your schedule monitor and control regimen. Develop collaborative relationships with project team members performing *Quality Audits* to prevent problems, and ensure project execution is conforming to established standards.

- **Management and Contingency Reserves:** Be aware of the impact budget has on the project schedule. If project reserves are being consumed at a high rate, or if it appears there are reserve shortages, understand the potential impact on schedules.

- **Critical Activity versus Critical Path Distinction:** The distinction between Critical Path and Critical Activities was shared earlier. This concept is worth repeating. Activity prioritization is based on multiple considerations. An activity on Critical Path is high priority. However, though a Critical Activity may not be on Critical Path, completion of the activity is vital to project success and must be prioritized, monitored, and controlled accordingly.

- **Electronic File Storage and Retrieval Standards:** A key activity in the Monitoring and Controlling Domain is information management. Understand organizational standards impacting file storage and retrieval. Ensure project data is capable of meeting rules and constraints.

- **Update Cycles:** Establish regular intervals when status is updated and reported. This sets expectations at both team and executive leadership levels. Reporting Performance at determined intervals, and sharing planned versus actual schedule results, results in the greatest project visibility. Avoid random reporting. It results in confusion and reduces overall reporting effectiveness.

- **Presentation Levels:** There are five levels of presentations. Each is designated for a specific audience. Each level provides greater detail, or a more granular overview of project status.

  o **Level 1: Executive Summary:** One-page summary. Generally includes a high-level summary of activities and major contractual and project related milestones.

  o **Level 2: Management Summary:** An extension of Level 1. Includes similar high-level summary. Generally 4 to 5 pages. May include drill-down reports on specific areas.

  o **Level 3: Publication Schedule:** Level of detail required to support a monthly report. Includes all major milestones, major project scheduling elements, and more.

o **Level 4: Execution Planning:** Shows activities over a one-week duration. Provides look-ahead schedule of three-weeks.

o **Level 5: Detailed Planning:** Provides detailed instruction and status to support short-term planning for the field. Details critical areas of concern, constraints, potential workarounds, etc. for activities normally requiring duration of 1 week or less.

- **Performance Measurement Baseline (PMB) Analysis**: We introduced the PMB earlier. Ensure schedule performance matches performance parameters spelled out in the PMB.

- **Status Review Meetings**: Status review meetings are held during Monitor and Control. They are scheduled in the Communications Management Plan discussed in-depth in Chapter 6. Project status is reviewed and reports are analyzed. Variance analysis to compare planned versus actual results is accomplished. Recommended cadence for conducting status meetings is *weekly*.

- **Activity Calendars:** *Activity Calendars* define working and non-working times for the project. The Project Scheduler confirms schedules are occurring as planned. *The Activity Calendar replaces the Project Calendar for actual schedule calculations.*

- **Variance Analysis:** The definition of variance analysis—comparing planned versus actual work or progress is important. Here are examples of variance analysis performed:

o **Actual Activity Duration:** How much actual time elapsed on each activity or Work Package started? Will the activity's actual duration meet the planned duration? If not, what corrective measures can be taken? Compare Actual Activity Duration to *Activity Original Duration*. This was the length of time allocated to the activity prior to any work commencing.

o **Activity Actual Finish Date:** Has actual completion of activities been validated? There is a common saying "trust but verify." Project Schedulers should trust activity completion reports. However, verify completed activities meet project requirements.

○ **Activity Actual Start Date:** Verify reported activity starts as accurate. Don't assume an activity started just because it was scheduled. Again—trust but verify. After determining the Activity Actual Start Date, you can better determine *Activity Remaining Duration*. This is the time required to complete the activity.

○ **Activity Actual Cost (AC):** Did AC meet the planned estimate? If not, how will cost overruns impact future scheduled activities?

Chapter 4 Summary

This chapter discussed Domain 3 of the PMI-SP Certification Exam. Schedule Monitoring and Controlling is the process of monitoring schedule progress to ensure project goals are met. Schedule analysis and reporting are keys to success. Proactively provide the right information to the right stakeholders at the right time to ensure the collaboration necessary to adjust and move forward. Finally, manage change or it will manage you.

We covered multiple concepts, definitions, and additional applications necessary to effectively monitor and control a schedule to meet project needs. Remember, this domain addresses 35% of all questions on the PMI-SP Certification Exam.

Chapter 5 addresses the Schedule Closeout domain. This is a short chapter, but still quite critical to project schedule success. Challenge yourself to complete Activity 4D. Activity responses are in Appendix A.

Peter's Real World Perspective #2

Determining and reporting where we have been and where we are progress reporting is useful. So are trend analysis and all EVM techniques. However, all of these methods tend to ignore perhaps the most important thing – what is it going to take to finish? Let's decompose this question into a couple of questions. These questions are most useful to ask at the Work Package level.

1) What do we need to know that we do not know today in order to finish?

2) Is the remaining duration for this element of the schedule realistic, or do we need to adjust it based upon our answer to 1) above? Do we need to adjust costs, resources, quality, and/or scope?

This conversation we are opening up should make you think of the quote "what got us here won't get us there". We need to be more forward looking:

- Determine what it will take to resolve current issues
- Devote more attention to risk identification and management, especially response strategies
- Identify hurdles and blockers and how to overcome these.

A schedule that is trending back to plan towards its PMB does not mean this positive trend is likely to continue – the opposite may in reality be true. Do not be lulled into comfort and complacency by the results of trend analysis, EVM and other methods. These are useful models but they are just that – models. Get real – THINK about what is really going on, and what it will take to finish. Mark Twain once said, "Common sense is very uncommon." Use your common sense.

Activity 4D: Schedule Monitoring and Controlling

Schedule Monitoring and Controlling Activity	Response
1. A dollar value tied to the estimated value of the work already accomplished on a project	
2. Level of detail required to support a monthly report. Includes all major milestones, major project scheduling elements, and more	
3. Defines working and non-working times for the project. Replaces the Project Calendar for actual schedule calculations	
4. Metric that shows how the schedule is progressing according to the plan. You are behind schedule if this metric is less than 1.0	
5. External group that reviews and approves/disapproves changes. Form if the project is large, or has a high-degree of competing stakeholder interests	
6. Takes Work Performance Data and formats it to provide useable schedule performance information that can be used by stakeholders	
7. *The #1 goal* of change management. Accomplish this goal by having a transparent change control system that is well communicated	
8. Calculation that shows the level of effort required to complete a project based on BAC or EAC	
9. One-page summary. Generally includes a high-level summary of activities and major contractual and project related milestones	
10. Initially assigned to define working and non-working times for schedule activities and resources; i.e., holidays, weekend schedules, etc.	
11. Industry standard used to measure planned versus actual schedule and cost performance. Provides current status snapshot of schedule and cost status	
12. One of three methods used to calculate a project's *Activity Duration Percent Complete*	
13. Share your findings with other project managers so they can take advantage of the knowledge gained over the course of a project	
14. Compare planned versus actual project results, look for variations, and address them	
15. Intended to ensure the project's standards are being followed and prevent potential problems from occurring	

Activity 4D: Choose from following:

A. To Complete Performance Index (TCPI)

B. Activity Calendar

C. SPI

D. Work Performance Information

E. Variance Analysis

F. Earned Value (EV)

G. 20/80 Rule

H. Lessons Learned

I. Change Control Board (CCB)

J. Level 1: Executive Summary

K. Project Calendar

L. Level 3: Publication Schedule

M. Quality Audit

N. Influence Factors that Cause Change

O. Earned Value Management (EVM)

Chapter 5: Schedule Closeout

The Closing Process Group finalizes activities to formally close out a project, contract, or phase. Two processes in the *PMBOK* support the Closing Process Group. Domain 4 of the PMI-SP Certification Exam Outline Content is Schedule Closeout. The Schedule Closeout domain is 6% of the examination. The focus of this domain is finalizing schedule activities, evaluating overall schedule performance against the original Schedule Baseline, updating Organizational Process Assets as necessary, and performing and sharing Lessons Learned.

Figure 5.1 provides the Closing Process Group steps used to define Schedule Closeout.

Figure 5.1 Closing Process Group Steps

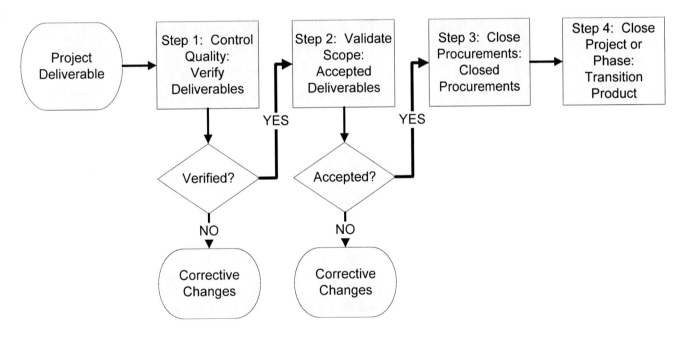

Closing Scheduling Implications:

Step 1: Control Quality: The first step to close out deliverables is performing a quality control inspection to determine if the product or service meets specifications outlined in the Project Management Plan. If so, move forward to customer acceptance. If not, corrective changes are submitted to eliminate defects found during inspection. The Project Scheduler plays key roles:

- **Schedule Impact:** If the deliverable is both validated and accepted (See Step 2), the Project Scheduler compares actual duration required to complete the deliverable versus the estimated or planned duration. This data impacts schedule performance metrics for the project.

- **Final or Interim Deliverable:** If the deliverable finalizes the project, the Project Scheduler begins work to finalize final schedule reports including EVM, variance analysis, Lessons Learned, and required reports to stakeholders. If the inspection supports an interim deliverable, the Project Scheduler integrates data into schedule models, determines impact on planned versus actual schedule performance goals, develops applicable presentations, and presents status. This is contingent upon acceptance in Step 2

- **Changes:** If the deliverable is not validated, the Project Scheduler analyzes the impact of any corrective changes required to the schedule and adjusts as required.

Step 2: Validate Scope: Customers evaluate validated deliverables and either accept or not accept results. This process requires a joint customer and team inspection the Project Scheduler is involved in. The ultimate goal of project quality is to *conform to requirements,* and provide a product/service *fit for use.* Step 1 accommodates conform to requirements. Step 2 evaluates fit for use. Key roles include:

- **Schedule Acceptance:** The Project Scheduler must gain acceptance for all scheduling components before final data can be analyzed and project scheduling models are updated.

- **Stakeholder Feedback:** The Project Scheduler solicits feedback from stakeholders to develop Lessons Learned and propose improvement ideas for future projects. Stakeholders may accept final or interim deliverables. However, that is not a guarantee they are happy with results.

- **Reports:** All reports initiated in Step 1 may now be finalized and shared as required.

Step 3: Close Procurements: All contracts and agreements are finalized and seller payments are initiated during this step. Again, the Project Scheduler is involved.

- **Contractual Schedule Acceptance**: Ensure seller met all required schedule considerations. The Project Scheduler provides this input.

- **Procurement Audit:** *Procurement Audits* are performed at the conclusion of each project. This activity analyzes the overall procurement process from planning to close to determine how future contractual performance can be improved. The Project Scheduler is a key participant.

- **Procurement Negotiations:** There are times when there are issues, disputes, claims, or settlements necessary. *Settlements* may occur if work is incomplete, or the contract was terminated early. The Project Scheduler provides valued input during these negotiations when schedule components are a factor.

- **Forensic Schedule Analysis:** We defined this concept in Chapter 4. To repeat--*Forensic Schedule Analysis* may be used for legal proceedings. This is sometimes a consideration when negotiations and settlements are an issue. Forensic Schedule Analysis is performed retrospectively with the goal of identifying true causes and impacts of schedule delays. The Project Scheduler may perform this analysis if circumstances dictate.

- **Claims Administration:** Many contracts include a *Claims Administration* clause. This guidance shares how sellers and buyers can formally process and communicate contract issues. The Project Scheduler may provide input if circumstances so warrant.

Step 4: Close Project or Phase: Close Project or Phase transitions the final product or service to operations, or formally closes out a project phase. The Project Scheduler adheres to formal schedule close-out procedures and is involved:

- **Transition Planning:** The Project Scheduler participates in transition planning to ensure transfer of project deliverables to operations as planned. Scheduling issues impacting transition are identified and addressed.

- **Lessons Learned:** Conduct Lessons Learned at the end of each phase, or minimally, at the end of the project. Lessons Learned support other project managers on future projects. This concept is discussed later in this chapter.

- **Final Reports:** The Project Scheduler finalizes schedule reports for stakeholders. This includes comparing final performance to the original Schedule Baseline and documenting variances to be shared during Lessons Learned.

- **Archive Final Schedule Files:** The Project Scheduler conforms to standard records management procedures. This action is discussed later.

Conducting Lessons Learned

Lessons Learned are a small time investment yielding big results. Lessons Learned may be referred to as "Post Mortem." Lessons Learned allow project stakeholders to evaluate a project in terms of what worked and what didn't. They also allow organizations to better prepare for future projects by embracing best practices, and avoiding pitfalls. Here are reasons to conduct Lessons Learned:

- **Assist Future Project Managers:** We often repeat the same mistakes over and over again. Lessons Learned point out common mistakes, and provide an opportunity for future project managers to learn how to best avoid those pitfalls. In addition, new ideas providing value are often discovered during execution of a project. Sadly many of these great ideas are lost. Lessons Learned provide an opportunity to share the wealth.

- **Validate Stakeholder Satisfaction:** Lessons Learned allow project teams to interact with customers, users, leadership and other key stakeholders to determine what worked and what needs improvement from their standpoint. As a case in point, let's say there was a customer who worked with you throughout the project and was very supporting. At the end of the project, their needs were not met. Lessons Learned allow you to determine what went wrong from this customer's standpoint, and address issues in future projects. If you don't address the issue now, support from this customer may erode on future projects.

- **Next Steps:** Oftentimes, a single project is a journey leading to new ideas and opportunities to go from good to great. Use Lessons Learned as an opportunity to discuss what you learned, and identify opportunities to take next steps while the project is still fresh on your mind!

Figure 5.2 provides an easy to follow template on how to maximize Lessons Learned.

Figure 5.2 Lessons Learned Template

Question	Comments
1. What went well?	• Always begin with a positive question. People love to share their successes. • Search for best practices, great ideas, potential opportunities, etc. resulting from the project.
2. What can we improve? (Note the Wording!)	• DO NOT ask what went wrong. People are resistant to share where they failed or came up short. • DO ask how we can improve. Address this question from a "Good to Great" standpoint. • Let people know they did well, but allow stakeholders to offer suggestions on what to improve next time.
3. How can we improve?	• This section is a continuation of question #2. For each improvement idea, spend some time determining how to turn the great idea into reality. • Try to pick one or two things to apply to the next project. Gain team commitment to these improvements.

Schedule File Archiving

There are final steps required to successfully close a project. Archiving requirements must be considered. The majority of archiving requirements are referred to in the *PMBOK* as Organizational Process Assets updates.

- **Schedule Files:** The Schedule Management Plan should be archived for use by others in the future. Final schedule model instances and presentations, status reports, and schedule change logs should be archived and maintained for analysis and benchmarking on future projects.

- **Contractual Files:** Contractual documents, in particular those impacted by or impacting project schedules, should be maintained and archived. These documents become critical if Forensic Schedule Analysis is required.

- **EVM:** Archive final EVM reports. Not all projects attain 100% EV. Use this data to provide Lessons Learned input and pave the way for improved future scheduling performance.

- **Risk:** Archive documentation that identified risks, probability and impact data, responses, etc. Risk Management is discussed in Chapter 7.

- **Standards, Processes, and Company Policy:** What changes, additions, deletions, etc. are required to improve future schedule performance?

- **Performance Measurement:** Did guidelines work as planned? Are changes/alterations required?

- **Templates:** Are current templates meeting project scheduling needs of the organization? Are improvement/additions required?

- **Work Authorization Systems:** *Work Authorization Systems* are procedures dictating how and when work can progress. Did systems serve the project well, or are changes/adjustments required?

- **Configuration Management:** Did configuration management methods to control change to project functional and physical characteristics work as planned? Changes required?

- **Estimation Techniques:** Do current estimation techniques yield accurate schedule results? Changes required?

- **Historical Information:** Did available historical information assist project scheduling efforts? Additions or updates required?

Chapter 5 Summary

This chapter discussed Domain 4 of the PMI-SP Certification Exam. Schedule Closeout ensures activities to finalize schedule activities, evaluate project schedule performance, document Lessons Learned, ensure customer acceptance, and successfully transition deliverables to operations in a timely manner occur.

This was a short but important chapter. Remember, this domain addresses 6% of all questions on the PMI-SP Certification Exam.

Chapter 6 addresses the Stakeholder Communications Management domain. Challenge yourself to complete Activity 5. Activity responses are in Appendix A.

Activity 5: Schedule Closeout

Answer the following true or false questions to test your knowledge.

Question	True or False
1. Verification of project deliverables occurs during the Validate Scope process	
2. Control Quality ensures the project conforms to requirements. Validate Scope ensures fit for use	
3. Forensic Schedule Analysis may be used for legal proceedings and is performed retrospectively	
4. Quality Audits analyzes the overall procurement process from planning to close to improve future project contractual performance	
5. The customer is required to verify deliverables to determine if corrective changes are required	
6. Settlement guidance shares how sellers and buyers can formally process and communicate contract issues	
7. Lessons Learned should be optimally conducted at the end of each phase	
8. The Close Project or Phase process occurs once during every project	
9. Lesson Learned sessions should always begin with a positive question	
10. Work Authorization Systems are procedures that dictate how and when work can progress	
11. The final step in the Closing process Group is to Close procurements	
12. The Schedule Management Plan should be archived for use by others in the future as part of Enterprise Environmental Factor updates	

Chapter 6: Stakeholder Communications Management

Stakeholder Communications Management is Domain 5 of the PMI-SP Certification Exam. The Stakeholder Communications Management domain is 14% of the examination. This chapter covers key concepts in this domain. Our primary reference is *PMBOK* Chapters 10 and 13.

Project Communications Management

Let's begin with Project Communications Management. A three-step Project Communications Management Process is outlined in Figure 6.1.

Figure 6.1 Project Communications Management Process

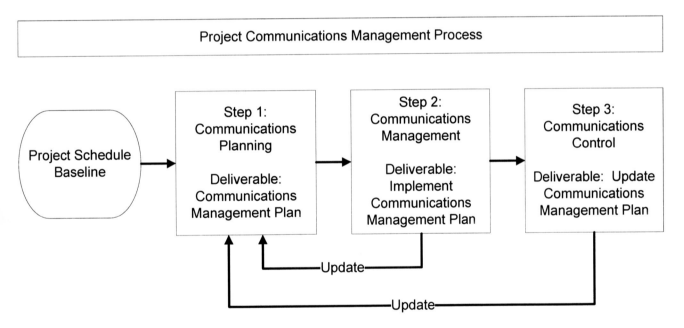

Communications Planning

Communications Planning supports the end-to-end communications needs of the project. PMI states 90% of all project activities are impacted directly or indirectly by communications. Communications is the glue that holds the project together. The Project Scheduler uses appropriate methods and techniques to maintain visibility of the project schedule. Here is a list of topics.

- Communications Management Plan

- Calculating Communications Channels

- Communications Model

- Tools and Techniques

The Communications Management Plan: This is a key document supporting the Schedule Management Process. Defines who needs to receive schedule related communications to include information, responses, status, meetings, etc. Primary contents:

1. **What:** What information needs to be communicated?

2. **Who:** Who must we communicate with? Who owns the communications item? Who authorizes communications? Address stakeholder communications requirements, including who receives information, and who is responsible to ensure information is communicated.

3. **Why:** Why is the communication important? Why should the receiver care about the communication? What is the value proposition?

4. **How:** What media, methods, language, and technology are used to communicate? Are there templates, formats, etc.? How is version control addressed? Flowcharts of the process may be included for clarity.

5. **When and Where:** When should communication occur? What is the optimal frequency for communications? Where will communications occur?

The following additional areas should be included in the Communications Management Plan:

1. **Change Management:** How Integrated Change Control is accomplished.

2. **Escalation Management:** How escalations are addressed in the project.

3. **Glossary:** Specific definitions and terms required to manage the project. Include common acronyms.

4. **Resources Required:** Resources allocated for communication activities.

5. **Updates:** How Communications Management Plan is updated.

6. **Constraints:** Legislative, regulatory, technology, or organizational constraints.

Communications Channels: Know how to calculate the number of communications channels. The formula:

> **Communications Channels = n(n-1)/2**
>
> **If there are 8 stakeholders**
>
> **8(8-1)/2 = 28 channels**

In this instance, 28 different channels of communications exist. In other words, there are potentially 28 different interpretations of status. The Project manager must control communications. The Project manager's goal is to filter rumors, provide, and maintain the reality of the project.

Communications Model: Understand the communications model. See Figure 6.2.

Figure 6.2 Communications Model

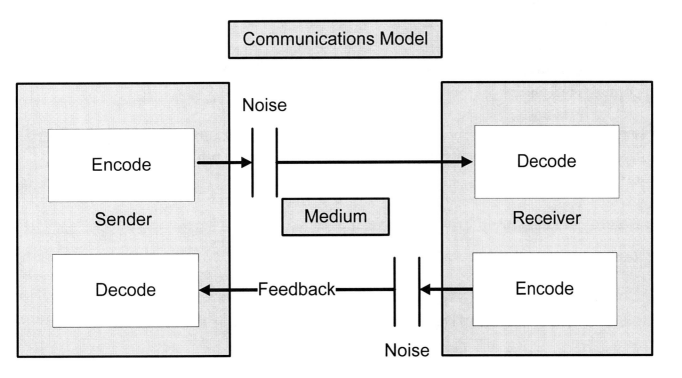

- **Sender:** The sender is responsible to **encode** the message and selects the proper **medium** to get it to the receiver. Examples include e-mail, fax, face-to-face, etc. The sender may use numerous communications methods or technology to encode.

- **Receiver:** The receiver is responsible to **decode** the message and select the proper **medium** to provide feedback. The receiver may use numerous communications methods or technology to decode.

- **Feedback** is the primary purpose of communications.

- **Noise** factors distort or interfere with understanding, transmission, or block the message. PMI refers to noise as *communications blockers*. The goal of communications management is to overcome noise factors and enhance the flow of communication. *The most likely result of noise (communications blockers) is conflict.*

Communications Planning Tools and Techniques—Communications Methods: Communications methods best suited to deal with diverse stakeholder groups include:

- **Interactive communication:** Two or more parties; multi-directional exchange of information.

- **Push communication:** Send out with no certification information was received or understood.

- **Pull communication:** Information available to stakeholders at their discretion; i.e. share point or web site.

Communications Planning Tools and Techniques—Communications Technology: Methods used to transfer information impact choices of communication. Understand "technology factors" affecting the project:

- **Urgency of need for information**: Need it now?

- **Technology availability**: Systems in place?

- **Ease of use**: Technology choices suitable for all?

- **Sensitivity and confidentiality of information**: Security measures required?

- **Project environment**: Collocated or virtual team?

Communications Management

The Communications Management Plan shares information to stakeholders *in a timely manner*. Communications is an art and a science. Things to keep in mind when communicating include:

- Non-Verbal Communications: 55% of communication is non-verbal. That is a majority!

- Paralingual: Much is said by the tone of a voice.

- Active Listening: Look for receiver confirmation they are listening. Ask for agreement or clarification.

- Feedback: Determine if the message sent was the message received. Note that feedback may not always be positive.

Primary Methods of Communication

A project manager must make careful choices when communicating. There are four primary methods of communication to include:

1. Formal Written

2. Formal Verbal

3. Informal Written

4. Informal Verbal

- *Formal written* includes correspondence meant for *public consumption*. Includes documents or verbiage key stakeholders need access to. Formal correspondence is always a *matter of record*.

- *Informal written* occurs when communications is *not meant for public consumption* (*Targeted limited number of stakeholders*). Informal communications is personal. It is *not normally a matter of record*.

- Meeting agendas, minutes, status reports, etc. are Formal Written. Conducting a meeting is classified as Informal Verbal. This rule holds true even if the meeting discusses critical issues.

- "Presentations" are generally regarded as verbal.

- Counseling and appraisals are a two-step process. Step 1 is informal verbal discussion. Step 2 is formal written acknowledgement.

- Treat memos and notes as informal. This includes email as well. When you see team, think informal.

- **Hint:** If distance or complexity is mentioned, use formal and written.

The best communication technique for conflict resolution is face-to-face. In addition, when issues occur, address them IMMEDIATELY.

Figure 6.3 provides a quick breakout of communications types. Use the communications type best suiting the issue, audience, and subject matter.

Figure 6.3 Communications Types

Formal Written:	Informal Written:
<ul><li>Project Charters, Plans, Status Reports, etc.</li><li>Long distance communications</li><li>Communications sharing a complex problem</li><li>*Documentation* of counseling and performance appraisals</li><li>Formal requests for baseline changes or resources</li><li>Meeting agendas and minutes</li><li>Used to target communications to senior management</li></ul>	<ul><li>Memos and notes</li><li>Communications for project *team*</li><li>E-Mail (You may use as Formal Written—majority of e-mail falls in this category)</li></ul>

Formal Verbal:	Informal Verbal:
• Presentations—Pre-Baseline, Baseline, status, etc. generally to senior management • Though you PowerPoint, the goal of a presentation is to share information verbally	• *Conducting* meetings, counseling, performance appraisals etc. Conducting = Verbal • Team conversations • Conversations at non-formal settings

Communications Control

Communications Control is the process of monitoring and controlling communications throughout the project to ensure optimal information flow. Activities the Project manager and Project Scheduler need to be aware of:

- **Updates and Version Control**: Communications needs of the project change over time. Update the Communications Management Plan on a periodic basis, share changes, answer questions, address communications issues, and gain commitment of stakeholders to follow the plan.

- **Issues:** Issues management can win or lose stakeholders. Address issues impacting project scope, schedules, and costs proactively. Elevates awareness to relevant stakeholders and gain credibility.

  o Not addressing issues is an accident waiting to happen. An issues log provides status to stakeholders. The issues log should be comprehensive, current, and accessible. Each issue should be assigned to a single owner for resolution.

  o **Note**: *Unresolved issues = conflict and delay. Scheduling issues are the greatest issue causing conflict.*

  o **Work Performance Information:** Project Schedulers analyze Work Performance Data related to the project schedule. Work Performance Information is provided to generate of Work Performance Reports.

Project Stakeholder Management

There are a number of pertinent areas from Chapter 13 of the *PMBOK* under Project Stakeholder Management. Domain 5 lists a number of stakeholder engagement tasks to be aware of. Figure 6.4 provides an overview of four Stakeholder Management Processes.

Figure 6.4 Project Stakeholder Management Processes

Process	Goal	Major Deliverables
1. Identify Stakeholders	• Identify project stakeholders and roles • Determine stakeholders who impact schedule development and execution	• Initial Stakeholder Register • Stakeholder roles and responsibilities
2. Plan Stakeholder Management	• Use "Stakeholder Management Plan" to classify stakeholders • Define current commitment levels • Develop strategy to go from "current" to "desired" state	• Stakeholder Management Plan • Stakeholder strategies
3. Manage Stakeholder Engagement	• Implement Stakeholder Management Plan • Implement strategies to move from "current" to "desired"	• Effective Communications • Issues Management • Creation of "Issues" Log
4. Control Stakeholder Engagement	• Monitor and Control stakeholder activities • Manage issues to conclusion • Be aware stakeholder management is a continuous activity	• Effective Communications • Resolved Issues • Change/Update Stakeholder Register, Stakeholder Management Plan as needed

Stakeholder engagement is critical from beginning to end of a project. Some tips impacting Domain 5:

- **Interpersonal Skills:** Interpersonal skills are used to foster appropriate levels of shared accountability, responsibility, and ownership. PMI provides a robust list of 11 interpersonal skills to perfect to the maximum extent possible. Figure 6.5 outlines these skills:

Figure 6.5 Project Management Interpersonal Skills

Skill
Effective Communication: Understand communications channels and informational requirements
Leadership: Focus group efforts toward a common goal. Get things done through others
Coaching: Share talents, skills, competencies etc. with others
Motivation: Create environment to meet project objectives and offer self-satisfaction
Conflict Management: Handle, control, and guide to achieve resolution
Negotiation: Confer with concerned parties to make agreements acceptable to all
Political and Cultural Awareness: Use politics and power skillfully to achieve project objectives
Influencing: Share power. Get others to cooperate toward common goals
Decision Making: Apply right style to ensure effective decisions in a timely manner
Team Building: Help individuals bound by common purpose work with each other and independently
Trust Building: Help people develop mutual respect, openness, understanding, and empathy. Develop communication and teamwork

- **Foster Engagement and Relationships:** Include stakeholders in initial planning meetings to discuss schedule models, strategies, goals, issues, risks, etc. Continue to include them as the project progresses. Share methodology, stakeholder expectations, and solicit feedback. The best schedule management function is supported by stakeholders and managed by the Project Scheduler.

- **Train the Trainer:** Project manager should use their Core Team to the maximum extent. Perform overall schedule planning and management as a team. When possible, delegate responsibility.

- **Use the Stakeholder Register:** Identify stakeholders who influence scheduling of the project. A key aspect of solid project management is identifying stakeholders, defining expectations, and managing expectations. Determine tolerance levels. Use the Communications Management Plan to set up meetings, interviews, etc. to determine and manage expectations.

- **Use the Stakeholder Management Plan:** Identifying attitudes toward schedules and the project is critical. The Stakeholder Management Plan determines current attitudes, determines desired attitudes, develops strategies to guide attitudes in the direction you need them, and manage stakeholder expectations effectively. Project Schedulers provide input, and solicit recommendations to effectively manage stakeholders who impact overall schedule effectiveness.

- **Updates:** Project Schedulers work closely with the Project manager to ensure timely updates are made to the Stakeholder Register. Stakeholder roles change as the project progresses. Services of some stakeholders are no longer required, and new stakeholder needs occur.

Project Stakeholder Management: Key Concepts

A *Stakeholder Register* identifies project stakeholders. This document is completed by the Project manager and shared with stakeholders to ensure understanding and commitment. Project Schedulers have a major input to identify stakeholders impacting end-to-end project schedule planning and implementation. The Stakeholder Register should have a comments section to use for multiple purposes. Some comments may be simple clarifications of roles. Other pertinent comments may spell out specific expectations. Scheduling criteria, goals, methods, issues, etc. may be an expectation you need to share. An example of a Stakeholder Register is provided in Figure 6.6. **Note:** This is a template I developed and is not a PMI standard.

Figure 6.6 Sample Stakeholder Register

Stakeholder Register Format							
Stakeholder Segment:							
Name	Organization	Role	R	A	C	I	Comments

RACI Terms Defined		
	R	Responsible for doing work on the project
	A	Accountable for outcomes
	C	Consult as Subject Matter Expert
	I	Inform as the Project Progresses

Version:

A *Stakeholder Management Plan* classifies key stakeholders for the project. This document is completed by the Project manager. However, this document is not meant for wide distribution. It is managed by the Project manager, and shared with select team members only. The Stakeholder Management Plan lists key stakeholders, and categorizes them based on five "Level of Commitment Designators". The goal is to determine current states, determine desired states, and develop strategies to move stakeholders from current to desired states.

Figure 6.7 shares a sample Stakeholder Management Plan. This is not a PMI standard. This tool was developed by me.

Figure 6.7 Stakeholder Management Plan

Stakeholder Management Plan Format			
Name	Current State	Desired State	Strategy

Recommended Level of Commitment Designators	U	Unaware: Stakeholder is unaware of the project.
	N	Neutral: Stakeholder has yet to determine level of support.
	R	Resistant: Stakeholder does not support the project.
	S	Supportive: Stakeholder agrees with the project.
	L	Leading: Supportive and actively engaged in project.

There are two common methods used to perform a stakeholder/impact analysis. **Stakeholder analysis** is a process of systematically gathering and analyzing quantitative and qualitative information to determine whose interests should be accounted for throughout the project. Interests, expectations, influences, etc. are considered. Use a 2-step process described in Figure 6.8:

Figure 6.8 Stakeholder Analysis Process

Step	Action	Considerations
STEP 1	Identify Potential Stakeholders	• Identify roles, departments, interests, knowledge levels, expectations, and influence levels. • Key on stakeholders in decision making or management roles impacted by the project. • Examples: sponsors, team, customers, etc. • *Primary identification method is brainstorming initially. Additional stakeholders identified through interviews.*

Step	Action	Considerations
STEP 2	Identify Stakeholder Impact	• Classify based on interest and power. • Prioritize to ensure expectations are met and communicated. • May use a power/interest grid (See Figure 6.9). • Other versions include (power/influence), (influence/impact), and the salience model (Power, Urgency, Legitimacy).

Stakeholder Impact Models: Two most common methods to evaluate stakeholder impact are shared in Figure 6.9.

Figure 6.9 Stakeholder Impact Models

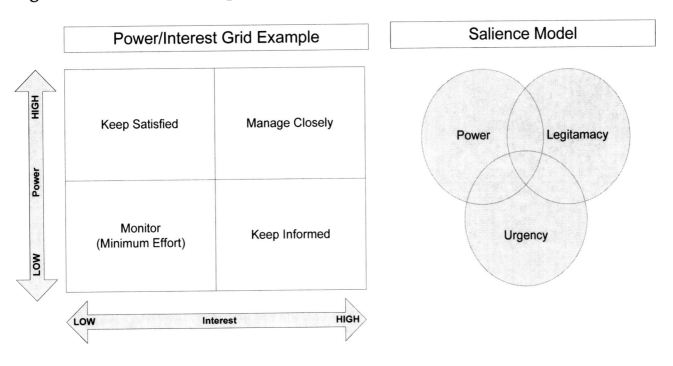

Power/Interest: Classify stakeholders based on power to impact the project, and interest level in the project. Determine the ideal quadrant for each stakeholder and take action based on the guidance in the grid. For example, a High Power and Low Interest stakeholder should be "kept satisfied". Provide only information necessary to keep them satisfied. **Note:** This is a tool for the Project manager and should not be shared.

Salience Model: Classify stakeholders based on their power, legitimacy and urgency. Power is power to influence the project. Legitimacy measures the stakeholder's essentiality to the project. Urgency correlates with level of interest or commitment. Develop strategies to manage stakeholders based on placement.

Chapter 6 Summary

This chapter discussed Domain 5 of the PMI-SP Certification Exam. Stakeholder Communications Management defines activities related to fostering relationships with stakeholders through effective communications, effectively maintaining stakeholder support, ensuring lines of communication are effective and continuous, and best practices to document and address scheduling issues.

Effective communications and stakeholder management can make or break a project. This domain addressed 14% of questions on the PMI-SP Certification Exam.

Chapter 7 addresses a variety of additional knowledge and skill areas you may encounter on the certification test. Challenge yourself to complete Activity 6. Activity responses are listed in Appendix A.

Activity 6: Stakeholder Communications Management

Directions: Match the definition to the responses. Answers are in Appendix A.

Stakeholder Communications Management Activity	Response
1. Documents current versus desired levels of stakeholder commitment and develops strategies.	
2. Factors that may distort and interfere with understanding, transmission, or block the message.	
3. Method of stakeholder classification that measures power, urgency, and legitimacy.	
4. Process used to update stakeholder management strategies and address issues.	
5. Primary method used to identify initial project stakeholders.	
6. Defines who needs to receive schedule related communications to include information, responses, status, meetings, etc.	
7. Document that identifies key stakeholders by role.	
8. Responsible to encode the message and selects the proper medium to get it to the receiver.	
9. Recommended method to manage a low power and high interest stakeholder.	
10. Information available to stakeholders at their discretion; i.e. share point or web site.	
11. Stakeholder who has yet to determine the level of support they are willing to a project.	
12. Result of transforming Work Performance Data into a more useable format.	

Activity 6: Choose from the following:

A. Pull Communications

B. Keep Informed

C. Communications Management Plan

D. Work Performance Information

E. Brainstorming

F. Neutral

G. Sender

H. Stakeholder Management Plan

I. Salience Model

J. Stakeholder Register

K. Control Stakeholder Engagement

L. Communications Blockers

Peter's Real World Perspective #3

This chapter provided several very useful models and methods for managing stakeholder communications – the 'science'. Do you know that the main reason projects fail to deliver their agreed scope is poor stakeholder identification and management? To effectively manage stakeholders we need to apply some 'art' in addition to the science.

Let's suppose we, the project team, are requesting a change to the project finish date due to a risk we just identified, and that we must "Accept" this risk (no other risk response strategy will work). How do we go about making this request while managing our stakeholders?

1) Be honest and transparent – where did the risk come from and why did the project team identify it very recently?

2) 'Tee up' the schedule change request for decision making:

   a. Are there any alternatives to adjusting the project finish date? If so, what are these, and what are the likely consequences of each alternative?

   b. If we adjust the project finish date, what are the likely consequences?

3) Facilitate the decision. Communicate the decision.

4) Implement the decision. Communicate progress and results.

Think of the project team as the project's delivery vehicle. When the vehicle goes off course and cannot deliver on time, then tell key stakeholders what happened and why, and give them choice – options for going forward. People want the truth, and they want choice. So give it to them – always.

Chapter 7: Additional Knowledge or Skill Area Requirements

Introduction to Project Management

Four areas to remember in Chapters 1 through 4 of the *PMBOK* include:

- Steps in PMI Framework
- Integrated Change Control
- Organizational Types
- Project Environments

PMI Framework: Consists of five Process Groups in order from Initiating Process Group through the Closing Process Group. See Figure 7.1

Figure 7.1 Five Process Groups

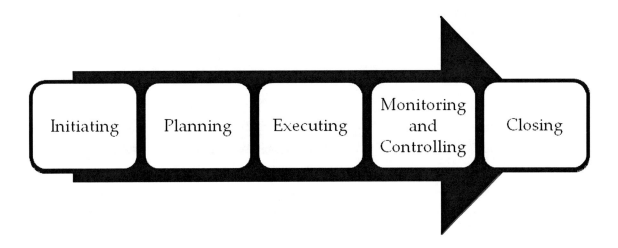

Integrated Change Control

Integrated Change Control Facts:

- Integrated Change Control procedures must be defined for every project. Procedures for reviewing changes include identifying new schedule risks or issues introduced by recommended changes.

- Create a Change Control Log. This log lists all change requests processed to support the project. It also provides status of changes including those approved and declined. The Change Control Log should be carefully reviewed by the Project Scheduler to determine scheduling impacts.

- Communicating approval or denial of recommended changes is a vital activity of Integrated Change Control. Approval or rejection of proposed changes likely impact scheduling considerations.

- Configuration Management is part of Integrated Change Control. It focuses on controlling changes to the functional and physical characteristics of the project's product or service. Configuration management was addressed in Chapter 2.

- A four-step process to effectively manage change:

  1. **Log and Evaluate:** Log all changes into the Project Change Log and assign a distinct tracking number. Evaluate each change for potential impact on time, cost, and scope. The Project Scheduler evaluates changes to determine potential schedule impact.

  2. **Determine Options:** Take a proactive approach to processing changes. Brainstorm options to integrate the change if approved into the overall Project Baseline with minimal disruption to project objectives? Schedule compression options as crashing or fast-tracking discussed in Chapter 3 are often options used to integrate a change with minimal impact on approved schedules.

3. **Process the Recommendation:** Changes are approved or rejected. Changes preventative or corrective in nature not impacting the Project Baseline are generally approved by the project management team. Changes impacting the Project Baseline must be approved by the Project Sponsor. Some projects have a *Change Control Board (CCB)*. This board consists of the Project Sponsor, key stakeholders, Project manager, and other key project team members. The Project Scheduler should be an attendee at the CCB when applicable.

4. **Share Results:** The project manager shares results of all change decisions. Some changes are accepted and implemented. When this occurs, Project Schedulers update schedule models, revise status reports, update applicable project documentation impacting project schedules, and ensure stakeholders are aware of schedule changes. If a change is rejected, the Project Scheduler needs to understand some stakeholders may become less committed and manage the impact accordingly. Effective change management is a key skill required to be an effective project manager or Project Scheduler.

Types of Organizations

There are three primary organizational models:

Organizational Structure	Key Attributes
FUNCTIONAL (Most Common Form)	• Each employee has one manager • Staff members grouped by specialty • "Silo" organizational model • Team members communicate up and down the silo
PROJECTIZED	• Team members collocated • Organization focus is projects • Project managers have high levels of authority and independence • Personnel assigned and report to project manager
MATRIX (The Default for PMI Questions)	• Blend of functional and projectized organizations • Resources borrowed from other functions • Team members report to two bosses; project manager and Functional Manager • Three Matrix types: Strong, Balanced, and Weak

Understand Project Environments: Major considerations impacting the Schedule Management Process include:

a. **Cultural and Social Environment:** Recognize how the project affects people and how people affect the project. Risk of stakeholders not buying-in to overall project goals increases if this environment is not addressed.

b. **International and Political Environment:** Knowledge of applicable laws and current political climates.

c. **Physical Environment:** How project impacts or is impacted by the surrounding physical environment.

Activity 7A: *PMBOK* Chapter 1 through 4 Review

Read the true or false questions below. Answers found in Appendix A.

Question	True or False
1. All change requests should be listed on a master Issues Log that supports the project.	
2. The Monitoring and Controlling Process Group follows the Planning Process Group.	
3. Configuration Management focuses on controlling changes to the project's product or service's functional and physical characteristics.	
4. Team members may be obligated to report to two managers in a Matrix organizational model.	
5. The focus of the Functional organizational model is on projects.	
6. "Silo" is a term often associated with the Matrix organizational model.	
7. Stakeholders are refusing to buy-in to overall project goals. In all likelihood, more time should have been spent on the Cultural and Social Environment.	
8. The PMI Framework consists of six interrelated Process Groups beginning with Initiating and ending with Closing.	

Project Quality Management

Project Quality Management is described in Chapter 8 of the *PMBOK*. Quality standards impact all PMI-SP domains. The *Quality Management Plan* supports end-to-end schedule management. Key outputs:

Quality Consideration	Quality Management Plan Entries
Quality Standards	Quality standards pertinent to the project. How team ensures they are met. Examples: • OSHA: Safety[8] • ISO 9000: Recommended quality standards[9] • Sarbanes-Oxley • Industry Standards and Codes
Responsibilities	Who helps manage project quality? What are specific responsibilities?
Quality Checklists	Steps that require specific verification. Quality Checklists support the project. These checklists are used in Control Quality.
Quality Metrics	Metrics to be measured? Ensure metrics are "SMART" (Specific, Measurable, Accountable, Realistic, Timely)
Targets	Current performance levels to improve upon from this project.
Process Improvement Plan	How waste and non-value activity are identified and reported.
Quality Assurance	Standards to be checked to prevent problems. How changes and preventative actions are addressed. How often Quality Audits are performed to check standards.
Quality Control	How inspections are managed. What is measured and reported. How changes and corrective actions are addressed.

---

[8] Occupational Safety and Health Administration (OSHA)
[9] International Organization for Standardization (ISO)

Project Human Resource Management

There pertinent topics covered in Chapter 9 of the *PMBOK* under Project Human Resource Management. They include:

- Human Resource Planning

- Motivational Theories

- Leadership Styles

- Leadership Style Applicability

- Negotiation Methods

- Conflict Management and Power

Human Resource Planning: A Human Resource Management Plan includes important information needed by a Project Scheduler. The plan includes:

- **Project Organizational Charts:** Uses OBS

- **Roles and Responsibilities:** Generally uses "RACI" method

ROLE	DEFINED
R	Responsible for doing work on the project
A	Accountable for project outcomes
C	Consult as a Subject Matter Expert (SME)
I	Inform as the project progresses

- **Staffing Management Plan:** When resources are onboarded and released

Motivational Theories: Motivation impacts stakeholder attitudes. Understand the following motivational theories and individuals responsible for each.

Motivational Theory	Key Points
Expectancy Theory	Employees believe effort leads to performance. Performance should be rewarded based on individual expectations. Rewards promote further productivity.
McGregor's Theory X and Y	All workers fit into 1 of 2 groups. Theory X managers believe people are not to be trusted and must be watched. Theory Y managers believe people should be trusted, want to achieve success, and are self–directed.
Maslow's Hierarchy of Needs Theory	Maslow stated motivation occurs in a hierarchal manner. Each level must be attained before moving to the next. (Physiological – Safety – Social – Esteem – Self Actualization)
Achievement Motivation Theory (Three Needs Theory)	David McClelland stated there are three needs that must be met for people to be satisfied. They include achievement, affiliation, and power.
Hertzberg's Theory	There are hygiene factors and motivating agents. Hygiene factors as salary, working conditions, benefits, etc. destroy motivation. They do not increase motivation. Motivating factors as responsibility, growth, and achievement increase motivation.

Leadership Styles: Leadership styles also impact stakeholder support of the Schedule Management Process. Each style is used on a situational basis.

Leadership Style	Definition
Directive	Tell people what to do.
Facilitative	Coordinate and solicit input of others.
Coaching	Train and instruct others how to perform work.

Supporting	Provide assistance and support as needed to achieve project goals.
Consensus Building	Solve problems based on group input. Strive for decision buy in and agreement.
Consultative	Invite others to provide input and ideas.
Autocratic	Make decisions without input from others.

Tuckman Model: Teams go through a step-by-step growth process. The Tuckman Model is a common five-step model used to depict growth of a team from the moment it is formed. This model is used to determine appropriate situation leadership styles.

Stage	Characteristics
Forming	Team meets and learns about the project. Roles are discussed. Expect hesitancy, confusion, anxiety, lack of purpose, and lack of identity. Productivity is low. Best strategy: "Tell."
Storming	Team begins to address work, technical decisions, and project management approaches. Conflict can occur which may disrupt the team. Leadership is challenged, cliques form, etc. Productivity decreases. Best strategy: "Sell."
Norming	Team members begin working together. They adjust individual habits to accommodate the team. There is open communication, purpose, confidence, motivation, etc. Productivity improves. Best strategy: "Participate."
Performing	Teams are independent, self-directed, and work through issues quickly. There is pride and trust. Productivity peaks. Best strategy: "Delegate."
Adjourning	Team completes all work.

Leadership Style Applicability: Each leadership style can be used to support a variety of situations. The table below provides common situations and recommended leadership styles.

Situation	Best Leadership Style
Team is forming. They need direction and task oriented information.	Directive, Coaching
Team is storming. There is conflict, frustration, and confusion.	Facilitative, Consensus Building, Consultative

Decision must be made quickly. Time is of the essence. There is little time for input.	Autocratic
Team is well established and skilled. They are in the norm or perform stages.	Supporting or Laissez-Faire (Hands off management style)

Negotiation: This is a key interpersonal skill. Use this in conjunction with influencing. Here are some important points:

- *Functional Manager* is the term associated with managers who manage project human resources needed. The project manager negotiates with Functional Managers to attain resources and support. Functional Managers may not always be "willing" providers. There are normally competing projects in an organization.

- The ability to influence multiple stakeholders to attain support is important. Note tips for effective negotiating.

Tips to Negotiate with Stakeholders
Understand and be able to explain the needs of the project. Be able to specifically spell out "what, why, who, where, when, and how factors" impacting schedules.
Be able to explain the business need for the project in an effort to gain support. The Functional Manager may not recognize project risks, benefits, etc.
Understand key stakeholders have other jobs to do. Understand their work situations. Be realistic.
Build a relationship. Assist stakeholders and create win-win situations.
Be flexible and willing to compromise.

Conflict Management: Conflict happens and must be controlled. Conflict stems from scarce resources, scheduling priorities, work styles, ground rules/norms, etc. There are situational methods to deal with conflict. Five primary methods:

- **Collaborate or Problem Solving:** Accommodate and incorporate several viewpoints to gain consensus and commitment.

- **Compromising or Reconciling:** Find solutions bringing some degree of satisfaction to each person,

- **Withdrawal or Avoidance:** Retreat or postpone a decision.

- **Smoothing or Accommodating:** Emphasizing agreement rather than differences of opinion. Try to calm people and encourage them to cooperate.

- **Forcing or Directing:** Push one viewpoint at the expense of another. Sometimes referred to "my way or the highway."

Power: Effective use of power is important. Five power sources a project manager may need to use:

- **Formal or Legitimate:** Power based on position. (#3)

- **Reward:** Giving rewards. (#1)

- **Penalty, Punishment, or Coercive:** Ability to penalize team members. (#5)

- **Expert:** The technical or project management expert. (#1)

- **Referent:** Sharing relationships to someone in a higher position. (#4)

Note: Reward and Expert power are the top two project manager powers. Reward power is inherent to the position. Expert power is earned. Numeric ratings denote importance of each power. For example, after reward and expert, which are top rated powers, formal power is rated third in importance.

Activity 7B: Project Quality and Human Resource Management Review

Read the true or false questions below. Answers found in Appendix A.

Question	True or False
1. A Theory X manager is one who believes people should be trusted and are self-directed.	
2. David McClelland is responsible for developing the Achievement Motivation Theory.	
3. According to Hertzberg's Theory, salary is a hygiene factor and responsibility is a motivating agent.	
4. Maslow created the Hierarchy of Needs Theory which places Esteem on the top rung.	
5. Training and instructing others is an attribute of the Consensus Building leadership style.	
6. Autocratic leaders generally make decisions with little or no input from others.	
7. A team entered the Storming phase. Facilitative and Consensus Building leadership styles are optimal in this phase.	
8. Performing is normally a step that a team achieves prior to Norming.	
9. A Functional Manager is a stakeholder who authorizes the project manager.	
10. Key metrics and performance objectives are defined in the Quality Management Plan.	
11. The primary tool used to accomplish Quality Assurance is inspections.	
12. Quality Checklists are developed for use in Control Quality and documented in the Quality Management Plan.	

Project Risk Management

Project Risk Management is a total project approach and execution of risk management. The high-level objective is to reduce impact of threats and enhance the impact of opportunities. These activities have a huge impact on the ability of the Project Scheduler to achieve scheduling objectives.

Project risk is defined as an *uncertain event or condition that may have a positive or negative impact* on project time, cost, or scope (quality).

Known risks are those previously identified and analyzed. The objective is to manage known risks. *Unknown risks* are those not yet identified. A key objective of risk management is to identify unknown risks so they can be planned and managed. Risk planning cannot be completed until all other planning is finalized. However, risk planning begins from Day 1 of the project!

A consistent approach to risk should be developed. A solid risk management function can reduce project problems by as much as 90%. There are six interrelated steps that support project risk management. Figure 7.2 provides an overview to serve as a guide.

Figure 7.2 Project Risk Management

Plan Risk

Step 1: Plan Risk: The project management team decides how to approach, plan, and execute the risk management activities for a project. The ultimate deliverable of this process is the *Risk Management Plan*. Risk planning is accomplished as early in the project as possible due to the potential impact of risk on all other processes.

The Risk Management Plan addresses risk for all aspects of the project including scheduling. The Project Scheduler provides valued input to ensure the plan addresses scheduling needs. Figure 7.3 provides an overview Plan contents.

Figure 7.3 Risk Management Plan

The Risk Management Plan becomes part of the Project Baseline and *must be approved by the Project Sponsor*. Recommended entries:

Risk Management Plan Consideration	Comments
Methodology	Approach to manage risk. Tools or data sources to be leveraged. Risk Breakdown Structure. (See Figure 7.4).
Roles and Responsibilities	Lead support, and team membership for risk planning. Define Risk Team.
Budgeting	How cost of risk is incorporated in the Cost Performance Baseline. How Contingency Planning occurs.
Timing	How often risk management is performed. Weekly is the norm.
Risk Categories	Risk categories impacting the project. A common method is assigning risk by time, scope, quality, and/or cost.
Definitions of Probability and Impact	Probability equals chances a risk event will occur. Impact equals consequences of the risk event to the project. Define both and determine how risks are prioritized using these indicators.
Probability and Impact Matrix	Tool used to determine how much effort to exert on a given risk. Generally differentiates risks by Risk Score as High, Moderate, or Low.
Stakeholder Attitudes, Tolerances and Thresholds	Levels of risk acceptable. • Attitudes impact tolerances, thresholds, and expected levels of commitment and support. • Tolerance is measure of risk levels management is willing to accept. • Thresholds are specific ranges, i.e., variations between + or – 5%.

Risk Management Plan Consideration	Comments
Reporting Formats	Reports, templates, documents used to record and communicate risk.
Tracking	How risk activities are recorded and shared. How risk process is audited. How Lessons Learned are captured and shared.

ey terminology:

- *Risk Tolerance Areas:* Areas key stakeholders are willing to accept risk. These areas should be identified.

- *Risk Averse:* Indicates stakeholder's unwillingness to accept risk.

- *Risk Thresholds:* Measure of risk stakeholder is willing to accept. Risk thresholds can be a percentage or a figure such as +/- 1 week, etc. Risks thresholds help determine responses to risk events.

- *Risk Utility:* Risk Utility describes a person or organization's willingness to accept risk.

Note: *Risk Breakdown Structure:* Many organizations use a Risk Breakdown Structure that lists risk *categories and sub-categories in hierarchical order* to help identify risks. This tool places risks in categories and defines specific risks applicable to the type of project being managed in that category. Figure 7.4 shares a Risk Breakdown Structure excerpt.

Figure 7.4 Risk Breakdown Structure Example

Financial			
Factor	Low Risk	Medium Risk	High Risk
Return	Forecast returns will be achieved within +/- 2%.	Forecast returns will be achieved within +/- 5%.	Returns on project are subject to major assumptions and wide variances.
Costs	Costs are set and not expected to exceed budget.	Cost estimates for some components are not known or quantified.	Cost analysis has not been done. Estimates are difficult to attain.
Budget Size	Sufficient budget is allocated.	Questionable budget allocated.	Doubtful budget is sufficient.

Budget Constraints	Funds allocated without constraints.	Some questions about availability of funds.	Source of funds in doubt or subject to change without notice.
Cost Controls	Well established and in place.	System in place, weak in some areas.	System lacking or nonexistent.

Identify Risks

Step 2: Identify Risks: This is the second step in Project Risk Management. The output is the initial *Risk Register* recording risks and their characteristics.

This process produces the first iteration of the Risk Register. The Risk Register should include risk, cause and triggers, Risk Owner, categories, and initial risk response. Key points:

- Each risk should have a single *Risk Owner*. The Risk Owner is validated and possibly changed during the Plan Risk Responses process. The project manager acts as the default Risk Owner if another Risk Team member is not identified. The project manager has an obligation to coach and train Risk Owners, and encourage their participation.

- There is no limit to the number of risks identified. The more risks identified the better! However, as discussed in Step 3—all risks are not equal.

- The Identify Risks process should include input from multiple stakeholders. Team members should be included in the process as well. Creating a sense of ownership with the stakeholders responsible for managing risk is critical. The Project Scheduler is a key contributor.

- The Risk Register serves as a key input for all Risk Management Process activities to follow. Risk Register creation is an iterative process. You continue to update the Risk Register as the project progresses. Version control is highly encouraged.

- *Risk meta-language* is a method enabling the project manager to effectively identify and describe risks. The goal of Identify Risks *is to identify as many negative and positive risks as possible.*

  o Negative risks can impact time, cost, and scope in an adverse way.

  o Positive risks can compensate for negative risks and allow for improved time, cost, and scope performance.

o   A three-step method to develop risk statements is illustrated in Figure 7.5.

Figure 7.5 Risk Metalanguage

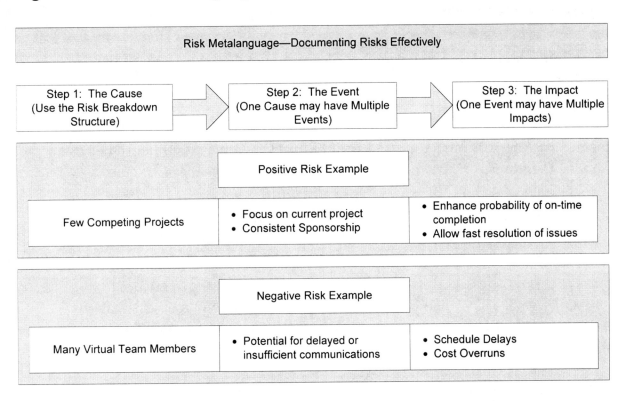

Tools and techniques to Identify Risks include looking at past, present, and future. Historical information allows project managers to compare current projects with past projects. This provides valuable information to identify risks, issues, and benefits. Creativity techniques identify future risks. *Testing Note: Tools and techniques to Identify Risks fall into three categories. They include past (Historical Reviews), present (Current Assessments), and future (Creativity Techniques).*

- **Documentation Reviews**: Read through project documentation. Is it clear and understandable? Do documented methods match project goals? Ensure documents are reviewed, edited, and clearly communicated to stakeholders.

- **Checklist Analysis**: Lessons Learned allow development of checklists supporting a variety of project types. The Checklist Analysis approach identifies potential risks and helps plan for them ahead of time.

  o   Checklist Analysis is a quick and simple approach to perform an initial high-level analysis of risks. Checklist Analysis doesn't identify new risks not on the checklist. This is a limitation.

- **Assumptions Analysis**: Assumptions are risks waiting to happen. By virtue of definition, "factors thought to be true without certain proof," they are dangerous. Assumptions Analysis needs to occur on every project. Assumptions must be validated or dismissed through analysis and research.

- **Diagramming Techniques**: Some common diagramming methods used for risk identification:

  o *Cause and Effect Diagrams*: Each cause to a potential effect is a risk factor to be considered. Alternate names for Cause and Effect Diagrams are Ishikawa Diagrams or Fishbone Diagrams.

  o *System of Process Flow Charts*: Project managers should learn how to map and analyze processes. Process flowcharts reveal how systems function, interrelate, and serve as a superb means of identifying potential risks.

  o *Influence Diagrams*: This method includes graphical representations of situations showing causal influences, time ordering of events, and other relationships between variables and outcomes.

- **Group Creativity Techniques**: There are tools and techniques managers need to understand and leverage on an everyday basis.

  o *Brainstorming: This technique is BOTH an Information Gathering Technique and Group Creativity Technique per the PMBOK.* Open forum where members generate ideas and solve problems. Facilitator logs inputs. Brainstorming is one method used for attaining expert input. *Refrain from evaluating responses during the brainstorming session.* This could impact success of this information gathering session.

  o *Delphi Technique: This technique is BOTH an Information Gathering Technique and Group Creativity Technique per the PMBOK.* Gain inputs and consensus through anonymous inputs. Reduces fear of reprisal. Delphi Technique is also a method to attain expert input.

    ▪ Surveys and questionnaires are two common methods used to solicit information.

    ▪ Share end results with all participants. Sharing information allows experts to expand their knowledge base. In addition, feedback generated often assists in identifying more risks than initially identified.

- Delphi Technique provides *social intelligence*. It reduces fear and intimidation factors. Delphi technique is sometimes termed Social Intelligence.

  o *Nominal Group Technique:* This technique is similar to brainstorming. Input is collected from a select group. This input is analyzed and rank ordered by the group.

  o *Affinity Diagramming*: This method uses the intellectual power of a group to place risks into categories. This is the *best method to use when it is believed that all possible risks were not identified.*

  o *Idea/Mind Mapping*: Consolidate ideas through individual brainstorming sessions into a single map to reflect commonality, differences in understanding, and generate new ideas.

- **SWOT:** Analyze opportunities and threats based on strengths and weaknesses.

  o Strengths and weaknesses are internal. Opportunities and threats are external.

  o Strengths lead to opportunities or positive risks. Weaknesses lead to threats or negative risks.

- **Interview:** This is a one-on-one conversation with key stakeholders or experts in a given field. A drawback is it takes time and is slow. *This is also an Information Gathering Technique.*

- **Root Cause Identification:** Same as Cause and Effect Analysis *Grouping risks by common causes can aid in developing more effective risk responses. This is also an Information Gathering Technique.*

- **Pre-Mortem:** Method used to identify potential risks before a project begins. Review your project and compare it to similar past projects. Determine what could go right or wrong with your project before it begins. Key sources of information include expert input, historical records, Lessons Learned, etc.

- **Prompt List:** Generic list of categories where risks may be found. List is used to "prompt" ideas and risk identification.

- **FMEA:** Failure Modes and Effect Analysis (FMEA) is a tool that identifies potential failure modes, determines effects of each failure, and seeks ways to mitigate the probability and impact of each failure.

- **Expert Judgement:** Identify risks as a team. *Include all stakeholders in the process*!

Tools and techniques to Identify Risks are defined in the Risk Management Plan, along with roles, responsibilities, and key stakeholders who should participate. Figure 7.6 and Figure 7.7 provide visual overviews of two key tools and techniques.

Figure 7.6 Delphi Technique

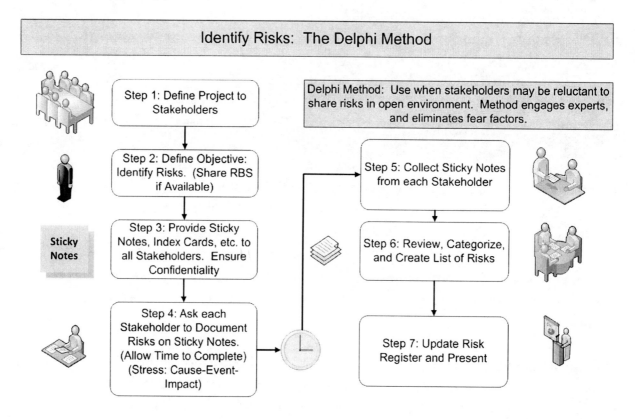

Figure 7.7 SWOT Analysis

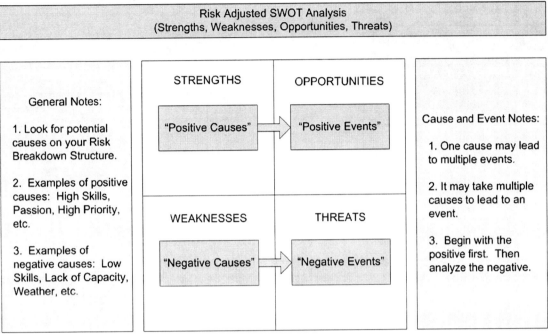

The output of Identify Risks is the *initial* Risk Register. The Risk Register becomes part of the formal Project Management Plan when approved and accepted.

The initial Risk Register is updated during subsequent processes in Project Risk Management and an input for all Risk Management Process steps that follow. Risk identification should be performed as early as possible in the project lifecycle. The earlier risks are identified, the quicker appropriate responses can be developed. Figure 7.8 shares an initial Risk Register.

Figure 7.8 Initial Risk Register

Risk	Cause and Triggers	Risk Owner	Category	Risk Response
		Initial		Initial
Initial Risk Owner and Risk Response are defined during Identify Risks. This information is revisited and validated during the Develop Risk Responses process.				

Testing Note: Note entries recommended for inclusion in the initial Risk Register.

- **Definition of the Risk (Event and Impact).** Note previous overview of Risk metalanguage

- **Causes and Triggers for the Individual Risk.** A *Trigger* is an early indicator a risk is about to occur. For example, if weather is a risk cause, the trigger may be a weather report, observation of incoming clouds, etc. A Trigger allows the Risk Owner to begin implementation of the risk response before the risk occurs.

- **Initial Risk Owner:** This is the stakeholder or team member who manages a risk throughout the project. It is recommended the Project Scheduler be the Risk Owner for schedule related risks.

- **Risk Categorization:** Categorization of risks allows project managers to sort risks. Scheduling may be a viable category allowing the Project Scheduler to isolate and key on schedule related risks.

- **Initial Risk Response:** The response to a risk. Goal is to reduce threats and increase opportunities. Step 5 provides more information on risk responses.

Qualify Risks

Qualify risks is a fast and effective method to prioritize risks on the Risk Register for further action as necessary. An overview of Step 3:

- **Risk Probability and Impact Assessment:** Evaluate and score all risks for probability (*likelihood*) and impact (*consequence* or *effect*). A consistent scoring system for risks should be used. Values for probability and risk are defined in the Risk Management Plan.

  - *Probability*: Probability is potential for a risk to occur. Scoring systems include percentages, or a numeric scale (1-5 for example). The assigned score is called a *Risk Rating*.

  - *Impact*: Defined as consequences the risk event has on the project. Impact should be linked to project objectives. Primary project objectives are scope, time, cost, and quality. Scoring can be based on many factors specific to the project. It is not uncommon to use weighted impact ratings assigning higher values to higher impact risks. For example, if schedule is the number one project priority, rate risks impacting schedule higher than others. The numeric score used for impact is also called a Risk Rating.

  - Multiply probability × impact to calculate *Risk Score*. Risk Score determines whether or not risk responses are developed. Risk Score also dictates levels of risk responses. Higher Risk Scores dictate higher levels of response detail and vice-versa. See example below (Figure 7.9). Risk A has the highest priority based on achieving the highest Risk Score. Risk D is the lowest priority risk despite having the highest impact score.

Figure 7.9 Risk Scoring Example

Risk	Probability Risk Rating	Impact Risk Rating	Risk Score
A	4	4	16
B	3	4	12
C	2	4	8
D	1	5	5

- **Probability and Impact Matrix:** Many organizations develop standard a Probability and Risk Matrix showing Risk Ratings and overall priority determinations. A Probability and Impact Risk Matrix can be simple or elaborate depending upon the prioritization methodology.

  o Tool is sometimes referred to as a *Lookup Table*.

  o Focusing on high priority risks is the best means to improve overall project performance.

  o Describing your Risk Rating criteria and developing a Probability and Impact Matrix reduces potential for bias and improves overall analysis. The Probability and Impact Matrix is part of the *Risk Management Plan*.

  o Review an example of a simple Probability and Impact Matrix (Figure 7.10)

Figure 7.10 Probability and Impact Matrix Example

Probability and Impact Scoring	Low Probability	Moderate Probability	High Probability
Low Impact	1	2	3
Moderate Impact	2	4	6
High Impact	3	6	9
Place all risks with score of 4 or below on "Watch List" Develop responses for all risks with score of 6 or higher			

- **Risk Data Quality Assessment:** Review data to determine probability and impact scores to ensure it is accurate and unbiased. Data used may not be sufficient to accurately define a Risk Score (probability × impact). If this is the case, annotate the risk as requiring further information to improve understanding before final analysis can be complete. *In addition, always correct a risk assessment that was impacted by bias.*

Types of bias:

- *Motivational Bias*: When stakeholders intentionally try to bias ratings one way or another.

- *Cognitive Bias:* Bias based on perceptions. "Perception is reality."

- *Bias may be desired.* It may be desirable to create bias toward high priority risks. For example, if schedule is the number one priority, rules that rate schedule risks higher than other types or categories should be established and implemented.

- Reduce bias by defining levels for probability and impact. Provide a Probability and Impact Matrix to reduce subjectivity of results.

- **Risk Categorization:** *Grouping risks by category assists in defining better risk responses.* This practice also allows for determination of common causes impacting multiple risks.

- **Risk Urgency Assessment:** The output of Qualify Risks is a prioritized list of risks. Questions include, "Which risks must be addressed immediately? Which risks can be placed on a Watch List as low priority?" A risk urgency assessment prioritizes risk response activities.

  o Risks requiring immediate responses are placed on an *Urgent List.* Risk Rating determines the level of urgency.

  o Risks not requiring immediate responses based on low Risk Score are placed on the *Watch List.* These risks are accepted in the near term. Responses are developed if Risk Score increases.

Figure 7.11 shows how the Risk Register evolves at the completion of Qualify Risks. Note key terms and concepts are underlined in *italics*. A number of updates are applied to the Risk Register at the end of this step.

Figure 7.11 Risk Register Update 1

Risk	Cause	Risk Owner	Category	Risk Response	Probability *Risk Rating*	Impact *Risk Rating*	*Risk Score*
		Initial		Initial	Add Step 3	Add Step 3	Add Step 3
The *Urgent List* for high priority risks.							
Draw the line on the Risk Register at conclusion of Qualify Risks. High priority risks fall on the Urgent List. Responses are developed. Low priority risks are placed on the Watch List. Responses are developed if Risk Score increases.							
The *Watch List* for low priority risks.							

Quantify Risks

Quantify Risks is the fourth step in Project Risk Management and keys on *numerical analysis*. Quantify Risks uses the updated Risk Register and provides an *objective* analysis of risk factors with potential to impact a project. Objectives of Quantify Risks:

- Quantify possible project outcomes and probabilities. Quantify Risks considers the *impact of multiple risks on desired project objectives or outcomes simultaneously*.

- Analyze pessimistic, most likely and optimistic scenarios using Three-Point Estimating methods. (Includes PERT). Note previous discussion in Chapter 3.

- Assess probability of achieving specific project objectives. Tools as Monte Carlo which provides specific timeframes or points when risk potential is highest, or Standard Deviation Analysis are quite effective for simulating probabilities of response.

- Identify risks requiring the most attention by quantifying their relative contribution to overall project risk.

- Identify realistic and achievable cost, schedule, scope, and quality targets in light of risk. *Determine Contingency Reserves required* for responses to risks.

- Determine best project management decision when some conditions or outcomes are uncertain. Make decisions based on objective, rather than subjective data.

Quantify Risks is not always accomplished. Qualify Risks is always mandatory. Considerations to perform Quantify Risks include:

- Cost, length, or relative priority of the project.

- Time and effort required versus benefits to be received.

- Complexity of the project and decisions to make a Go/No Go decision.

Expected Monetary Value is another method of quantifying contingency reserve requirements.

- **Expected Monetary Value (EMV)**: Method used to establish Contingency Reserve requirements for both budget and schedule. EMV is quantified by *multiplying probability times the best or worst case cost/time scenario*. Risk can be positive or negative. EMV provides the "Expected Monetary Value" of risk. Here is a sample scenario to illustrate EMV. Four risks impact Project XYZ. They are risks A, B, C, and D.

  - Risk A has a 30% chance of occurring and will cost the project $40,000. This is a negative risk. Using EMV, calculate required Contingency Reserves for Risk A (.3 × $40,000 = $12,000). Add $12,000 to the project budget.

  - Risk B has a 40% chance of occurring and will save the project ($10,000). (Numbers in parenthesis indicate positive risk. Subtract dollars from Contingency Reserve totals). This is a positive risk. Calculate (.4 × $10,000 = $4.000). Subtract $4,000 from the project budget.

  - Risk C has 75% chance of occurring and will cost the project $60,000. This is a negative risk. Calculate (.75 × $60,000 = $45,000). Add $45,000.

  - Risk D has a 50% chance of occurring and will cost the project $30,000. Calculate (.5 × $30,000 = $15,000). Add $15,000.

How much in Contingency Reserves is needed? Add up all negative and positive risk EMV totals. Total Contingency Reserve requirements equal $68,000. See Figure 7.12.

Figure 7.12 Expected Monetary Value (EMV)

Risk	Probability	Maximum Dollar Impact of Risk	Contingency $ Required
A	30%	$40,000	$12,000
B	40%	($10,000)	($4,000)
C	75%	$60,000	$45,000
D	50%	$30,000	$15,000
Total	Add $68,000 to project budget for Contingency Reserves.		$68,000

Figure 7.13 shows Risk Register updates based on the results of Quantify Risks.

Figure 7.13 Risk Register Update 2

Risk	Cause	Risk Owner	Category	Risk Response	Probability Risk Rating	Impact Risk Rating	Risk Score
		Initial		Initial	Update Step 4	Update Step 4	Update Step 4
					Update Step 4	Update Step 4	Update Step 4
Risk Register is updated at conclusion of Quantify Risks							

Develop Risk Responses

Develop Risk Responses is the fifth process in Project Risk Management. Primary objectives are to validate risk responses and Risk Owners identified during the Identify Risks process, or develop risk responses for risks on the Urgent List and assign Risk Owners if not previously accomplished.

Seven response strategies address risk. Three are for negative risks. Three are for positive risks. One response is used for both negative and positive risks. Each response is discussed in the tools and techniques section.

- *Risk Owners* are confirmed or assigned during Plan Risk Responses. Risk Owners develop responses, monitor risk status, and implement Contingency Plans and Fallback Plans if required. Risk Owners can be any stakeholder in the project.

- *Risk Action Owners* are individuals is by a Risk Owner to help implement approved risk responses.

- Primary responses to risks are referred to as either a *Contingency Plan* or a *Risk Response Plan*. You may develop a secondary plan should the Contingency Plan fail called a *Fallback Plan*. There may be times when Contingency Plans or Fallback Plans cannot be developed. The risk must be accepted when this is the case.

- Document *Secondary Risks* in the Risk Register as well. Secondary Risks result from a risk response. For example, a response to use a vendor to perform project work could lead to potential vendor management risks. Document vendor management risks as Secondary Risks. A Secondary Risk should *NEVER* have a higher Risk Rating than the primary risk it is associated with.

- *Residual Risks* must be accounted for. Residual Risks remain after a Risk Response Plan or Contingency Plan is implemented. For example, a response may address 80% of the risk impact. The remaining 20% represents the Residual Risk. Contingency Plans or Fallback Plans should be in place to respond to known Residual Risks. New Residual Risks may be discovered during a Risk Audit. If so, log the Residual Risk on the Risk Register and Perform Qualitative Risk Analysis.

The Develop Risk Responses step can lead to a Go/No Go decision. A No Go decision could occur if there are critical risks for which no responses can be developed.

- *The level of detail defined in a risk response should be based on the priority of the risk.* A high priority risk would warrant greater levels of detail than lower priority risks.

- Risk responses may lead to additional work causing the Schedule Baseline and/or Cost Performance Baseline to change. Solicit approval for this type of risk response from the Project Sponsor.

Tools and Techniques:

- **Contingent Response Strategies**: Events happen indicating a risk will occur. These are called *triggers*. When triggers occur, initiate the Risk Response Plan. For example, the project defines a contingency response strategy to order 10,000 spare parts from vendor B if vendor A misses planned shipments of spare parts by more than two days. The trigger occurs when vendor A misses the shipment times.

- **Strategies for Negative Risks and Threats**: There are four strategies addressing negative risks.

  - *Avoid (Avoidance):* Focus of this strategy is to *eliminate the cause* of the risk. Try to take action to ensure the risk does not occur. This is often accomplished by removing people and/or activities.

  - *Transfer (Transference)*: Response *transfers accountability and responsibility of a risk to a third party*. The third party actually performs the work or takes accountability. There is normally a cost incurred when using the transfer response. A prime example is the purchase of insurance.

  - *Mitigate (Mitigation):* Response takes actions to *reduce the probability of the risk occurring, or the impact of risk if it occurs*. An example is training. Try to reduce the probability and impact of employees performing poorly on the job by training them.

- *Accept (Acceptance):* Response entails taking no immediate action until the risk occurs. There are two types of acceptance strategies. One is *passive* and the other is *active*.

  - Acceptance is a response strategy appropriate for *BOTH* negative and positive risks.

  - A Contingency Plan or Fallback Plan may be developed for a risk you plan to accept. However, the response is not initiated until the risk occurs.

  - Acceptance is often the choice when risks are generated from external sources, or when risk responses are beyond control of the project manager.

  - *Passive Acceptance*: This type of acceptance occurs when no Contingency Plans are created to address the risk.

o *Active Acceptance*: Develop Contingency Plans to address the risk when it occurs. Active Acceptance is a solid option when necessary to convince risk adverse stakeholders that response plans for accepted risks are in place.

- **Strategies for Positive Risks or Opportunities:** There are four strategies addressing positive risks.

  o *Exploit (Exploitation):* Response takes action to *make a cause occur.* It may require additional time or resources to use the exploit response method. *This is the opposite of the avoid response.*

  o *Share (Sharing):* Response *enlists support of a third party to take advantage of the opportunities* presented by a positive risk event. Partnering with a third party allows both parties to share the benefits. *This is the opposite of the transfer response.*

  o *Enhance (Enhancing):* Response aims to *increase the probability of the risk occurring or the impact of a risk if it occurs.* Incentives are a common example of an enhance response. *This is the opposite of the mitigate response.*

- *Accept (Acceptance):* Acceptance is a feasible risk response for both negative and positive risks.

Outputs:

- **Project Management Plan Updates:** *Update Risk Register* and/or Risk Management Plan at the conclusion of Plan Risk Responses. Other key project management planning documents are also updated. Residual Risks and Secondary Risks are also documented.

- **Project Document Updates:** Risk integrates with many other areas. Updating project documents—to include schedule documentation-- is a potential result of Plan Risk Responses.

Figure 7.14 below shows specific Risk Register updates after Step 5:

Figure 7.14 Risk Register Update 3

Risk	Cause	Risk Owner	Category	Risk Response	Probability Risk Rating	Impact Risk Rating	Risk Score
		Update Step 5		Update Step 5	Update Step 5	Update Step 5	Update Step 5
		Update Step 5		Update Step 5	Update Step 5	Update Step 5	Update Step 5
Risk Owners and risk responses may be updated at conclusion of the Develop Risk Responses process. Risk Ratings and Risk Scores may be updated based on responses.							

Control Risk

Control Risk is the sixth step in Project Risk Management. Risk is an iterative process. Risk factors come and go and conditions continually change. Risk is not a one-time activity. The goal of Control Risks is to stay current. Control Risk:

- Ensures effectiveness of the Project Risk Management Process

- Tracks identified risks

- Monitors Residual and Secondary Risks

- Identifies, analyzes, and plans for new risks

- Keeps track of risks on the Watch List

- Reanalyzes existing risks as conditions change

- Monitors risk trigger conditions

- Implements Risk Response Plans

- Evaluates effectiveness of risk responses

- Updates Risk Register

- Submits formal changes when necessary to update Contingency Plans

- Responds to previously unidentified or unknown risks. Response is defined as a *workaround*

Tools and Techniques:

- **Risk Reassessment**: Control Risk often identifies new risks and requires reassessment of existing risks. In addition, outdated risks should be closed. *Risk Reassessment* also ensures new risks are identified project changes are made.

  o *Risk Reviews* analyze potential risk responses to determine if they are still appropriate. Risk Reviews may include changing the order or priority of risks, adjusting severity of existing risks, or monitoring Residual Risks.

  o Many events drive Risk Reassessments. Events include occurrences of unknown risks, evaluation of change requests, project re-planning, or conducting phase end reviews. Requirements for Risk Reassessment are included in the Risk Management Plan.

- **Risk Audits**: Risk Audits examine responses to risk and answer the question, "How did we do?" Risk Audits also measure the overall effectiveness of the Risk Management Process. Periodic Risk Audits should be performed to evaluate strengths and weaknesses of the overall Risk Management Process. Risk Audit requirements are identified in the Risk Management Plan. *Most Residual Risks are identified during Risk Audits.*

- **Variance and Trend Analysis:** Trends should be observed and deviations noted. Compare planned results with actual results.

- **Technical Performance Measurement:** The Quality Management Plan defines targets, metrics, etc. Technical performance measurement determines if actual technical performance achieved matches planned technical performance specifications.

- **Reserve Analysis:** Management Reserves or Contingency Reserves for risk may or may not be granted. If provided, the project manager manages reserves and ensures allocation *only* in the event of risk occurrence. There are some who look upon reserves as a great source for extras. Remember--Management Reserves are designated for *unknown unknowns* (Unknown Risks) while Contingency Reserves are designated for *known unknowns* (Known Risks).

- **Meetings:** Some portion of status meetings, or a separate meeting, is essential to address risks. Risks should be treated with importance, rather than a "by the way" subject. *PMI recommends weekly meetings to discuss project status.* Periodic meetings allow stakeholders to identify newly discovered risks throughout life of the project.

Outputs:

- **Risk Register Updates:** Outcomes of Risk Reassessment and Risk Audits may lead to updates. Actual outcomes from responses may require changes to the Risk Register.

- **Organizational Process Asset Updates:** Lessons Learned may lead to updated Risk Breakdown Structures. Other project management templates may require updates as well.

- **Change Requests:** Corrective or preventative change requests may be required to change Contingency Plans or Fallback Plans, or bring a project into compliance with the Project Management Plan. This is especially true when *Gold Platers* cause *Scope Creep.* Scope Creep is defined as changes to the Project Baseline not processed through formal Integrated Change Control. A Gold Plater is the name given to the individual or group that created Scope Creep.

Activity 7C: Project Risk Management

Directions: Match the definition to responses provided. Answers in Appendix A.

Risk Management Definition and Concept Activity	Response
1. Provides reserves to support risk identified on the Risk Register	
2. The primary focus of Quantify Risks	
3. Risks that may result directly from implementing a planned Contingency Plan	
4. A document that defines methods a project will employ to manage risk	
5. May be required to request additional reserves for a newly identified risk response	
6. A risk response that enlists the support of third parties to achieve an opportunity	
7. Risks that remain after implementing a planned Risk Response Plan. They must be accounted for on the Risk Register	
8. Lists risk categories and sub-categories in hierarchical order to help identify risks	
9. A process that identifies new risks, reassesses current risks, and closes out risks that are no longer applicable	
10. Tool that calculates risk contingency requirements by multiplying the probability of a risk times its potential dollar impact	
11. A risk response that aims to reduce the probability and/or the impact of a threat	
12. The primary focus of Qualify Risks	
13. The product of risk probability times risk impact	
14. Examines and documents the effectiveness of risk responses and the overall Risk Management Process	
15. A document used to document project risks throughout the duration of the project	
16. Compares project technical accomplishments to the schedule defining when technical achievement is required	

Activity 7C: Choose from the following:

A. Share

B. Risk Audit

C. Risk Reassessment

D. Residual Risks

E. Secondary Risks

F. Change Requests

G. Risk Register

H. Contingency Reserves

I. Technical Performance Measurement

J. Risk Management Plan

K. Probability × Impact

L. Probability and Outcomes

M. Expected Monetary Value (EMV)

N. Risk Breakdown Structure (RBS)

O. Risk Score

P. Mitigation

Project Procurement Management

Sometimes internal resources are not available to accomplish project goals. Projects may require external sellers to provide labor, expertise, equipment, supplies, materials, or other resources. Procurement impacts project schedules. Project Schedulers need to be aware of and participate in the project procurement process. Figure 7.15 provides an overview of the end-to-end procurement process. Understanding where schedules are impacted enhances chances for project success.

Figure 7.15 Project Procurement Process

Project Procurement Management

| Step 1: Plan Procurements

Output: Procurement Management Plan | Step 2: Conduct Procurements

Output: Final Contract | Step 3: Control Procurements

Output: Status and Changes | Step 4: Close Procurements

Output: Final Deliverables and Closed Contracts |
| --- | --- | --- | --- |

Step 1: Plan Procurements: The "Plan Procurements" process produces a Procurement Management Plan that guides the end-to-end procurement process. Project Schedulers need to participate in completion of this plan to ensure potential schedule support areas are addressed. Four distinct outputs are included in this plan.

- **Make or Buy Decision:** Management wants to ensure procurements are necessary. Project Schedulers may need to justify why internal resources cannot meet project schedule needs.

- **Statement of Work (SOW):** The procurement SOW needs to be detailed to the point where sellers can submit reasonable proposals to offer their services. The Project Scheduler ensures the SOW supports the specific needs of the schedule.

- **Contract Type:** Different types of contracts offer advantages and disadvantages to buyers and support varying project needs. Three common contract types are described in Figure 7.16 below.

Figure 7.16 Contract Types

Contract Type	Condition	Applicable Procurement Document	Risk Taker
Fixed Price (FP)	You have a detailed plan the seller must follow.	Invitation for Bid (IFB)	Seller
Cost Reimbursement (CR)	You know functionality, but do not have expertise to develop a plan.	Request for Proposal (RFP)	Buyer
Time and Material (TM)	You have a quick requirement to satisfy. Generally not complex.	Request for Quotation (RFQ)	Seller

- **Procurement Documents:** Types of procurement document are addressed in Figure 7.16 above. Procurement documents are utilized in bid and proposal activities. Most procurement documents are designed for a specific type of contract.

- **Source Selection Criteria:** The Project Scheduler provides input to source selection criteria used to select the winning proposal. Key scheduling success criteria should be part of the criteria. Note the same selection criteria must be used to evaluate all seller proposals.

- **Risk:** Sellers assume risk for a Fixed Price Contract which benefits the buyer. The buyer assumes risk for Cost Reimbursement and Fixed Price contracts. Project Schedulers need to be aware of contract risks and monitor them closely as the procurement process unfolds.

Step 2: Conduct Procurements: Conduct Procurements is the process of gathering proposals, selecting sellers, and finalizing a procurement contract. Project Schedulers need to ensure all contract schedule requirements are included in the contract and determine how and when they can interface with sellers.

Step 3: Control Procurements: Project Schedulers ensure all contract requirements impacting the schedule are met. Information from sellers is attained to allow for completion of scheduling status inputs, and schedule model presentations. If corrective changes are necessary, the Project Scheduler ensures submission through Integrated Change Control. Contract changes may be required to be submitted through a *Contract Change Control System*. This change management methodology becomes a subset of the project's Integrated Change Control process and addresses specifics required to change a contract specific.

Step 4: Close Procurements: Close Procurements was covered in Chapter 5. As a review, all contracts and agreements are finalized and seller payments initiated during this step. The Project Scheduler is involved in Contractual Schedule Acceptance, Procurement Audits, Procurement Negotiations, Settlements, Forensic Schedule Analysis, and Claims Administration.

This is the final section of this chapter. Challenge yourself with a procurement "fill in the blank" activity.

Activity 7D: Project Procurement Management

Fill in the blanks to test your knowledge. Responses are in Appendix A.

Question/Statement	Response
1. There are _____ steps in the end-to-end Project Procurement Process	
2. The procurement _____ should provide enough information for a seller to submit a proposal	
3. Source selection criteria should be applied _____ to all seller proposals	
4. Justification why internal resources cannot meet project schedule needs are include in the _____	
5. A _____ contract outlines specific deliverable requirements places risk on the seller	
6. A _____ contract is used when you are buying expertise you need to complete a deliverable	
7. A _____ contract would be used for a quick requirement that is not overly technical	
8. Three types of procurement documents are an IFB, RFP, and _____	
9. Procurement settlements occur during the _____ process of project procurement management	
10. Generally, changes to a procurement contract are processed through a _____	

Chapter 7 Summary

Chapter 7 included a variety of additional topics impacting the PMI-SP Certification Exam. Key topics included Process Groups, organizational structure, Integrated Change Control, Quality Management, Human Resource Management, Risk Management, and Procurement Management.

The PMI-SP Certification Exam's primary focus is Project Time Management. However, the Project Scheduler needs to appreciate how all aspects of the project impact the schedule. This chapter addressed many of those interfaces.

We developed a 150-question practice test designed to better prepare you for the real test. The Appendices list commonly used acronyms, and a Glossary of terms with references to the chapter where they were introduced.

Thank you for purchasing this book. We hope you are successful in attaining the PMI-SP certification. I can be reached at dan@P17group.com. Feel free to reach out to me if I can be of assistance to answer any questions you may have. In addition, we invite you to visit our website at www.P17group.com.

Thank you again and good luck.

APPENDIX A: Activity Responses

Activity 1: Introduction to Project Scheduling

Introduction to Project Scheduling Activity	Response
1. Activities planned at high-level pending information needed to plan them later in greater detail as the project progresses.	F
2. The path with the longest total duration on a project network diagram. Duration depicts total time required to complete a project.	J
3. The documents that contains requirements in the form of User Stories used in Agile Project Management.	M
4. Uses buffers to show points in the project network diagram where delays or additional time or resources are required.	C
5. The prevalent method used in modern scheduling tools. Allows you to calculate total duration, critical path, and early start and early finish dates.	I
6. A method where you plan in detail activities that are known and understood and delay planning on successor activities until more information is understood.	A
7. Specific outputs from a schedule model used to communicate key data to be used for analysis, course correction, decision making, etc.	G
8. Acknowledged on the project Resource Breakdown Structure as additional resources required to complete a project activity due to uncertainties.	B
9. Add time to the end of the project to account for a variety of uncertainties that may be identified while planning a project.	L
10. Copy of a schedule model. Provide a variety of presentations such as critical path analysis, resource data, and activities started and completed, etc.	H
11. Dynamic representation of a plan for executing project activities. Applies a selected scheduling method and uses the scheduling tool.	K
12. Normally an automated application that helps perform schedule network analysis to generate instances of a project schedule.	D
13. Used for scheduling activities in a project plan. Precedence relationships between activities are represented by circles connected by one or more arrows.	E
14. Define the role, need, and value proposition. Additionally outline acceptance criteria necessary for the team to attain.	N

Activity 2: Schedule Strategy

Schedule Strategy Challenge	
Question	**Response**
1. A hierarchical organizational chart that depicts the top-down organizational model for the firm	OBS
2. Any tangible, measureable output that the project will produce. Generally, key product or service attributes that satisfy project goals and objectives	Deliverable
3. Hierarchical decomposition of the total project scope required to produce a required product or service	WBS
4. Shows activity relationships and dependencies and allows for eventual calculation of critical path and creation of the Schedule Baseline	Project Network Diagram
5. Establishes and shares applicable policies and procedures necessary to plan, execute, control, and manage the project schedule throughout the project's lifecycle	Schedule Management Plan
6. Considerations include organizational policies and procedures, standard project management tools and templates, and historical information, such as Lessons Learned	Organizational Process Assets
7. Set of formal procedures used to identify, document, and manage the functional and physical characteristics of a project	Configuration Management
8. The process of breaking out project scope from a high level to lower level activities and Work Packages	Decomposition
9. The process of reviewing planned versus actual progress, identifying problems early, and being able to identify root causes	Variance Analysis
10. Allows you to describe the details or attributes of each Work Package without adding additional complexity to the WBS	WBS Dictionary
11. Key events or points in time that must be met to achieve project goals and objectives. Have no duration and no resources assigned	Milestones
12. Tool and technique to surround yourselves with those who can help you successfully plan and execute a project schedule	Expert Judgement

13. Initial document that authorizes a project to enter the planning stage approved by Project Sponsor	Project Charter
14. The unique numeric designator assigned to each activity and Work Package on a WBS	Code of Account Identifier
15. The approved and accepted version of the project schedule included in the Project Management Plan	Schedule Baseline
16. A numeric designator summing a team members potential work output derived from estimating skill levels and availability	Productivity Index
17. Considerations include acknowledgement of the organization's structure, systems, and culture. In addition, includes standards and regulations potentially impacting a project	Enterprise Environmental Factors
18. Deming perfected the work of Shewart and developed a concept that drives project management methodology today	PDCA

Productivity Index Bonus Question	
An activity requires 5 days to complete assuming a full-time resource with high skill sets. You have assigned a resource that has a skill rating of .75 and an availability of 80%. How long will this resource require to complete the 5-day activity?	8.33 Days

Activity Solution		
Skill	0.75	
Availability	80%	
PI	0.60	
Solution	8.33	5 Day/0.60

Activity 3A: Schedule Model Creation Steps 1-4

Schedule Model Creation Steps 1-4 Activity	Response
1. The first step in the schedule model creation process where you determine start and end dates, key points of time where deliverables must be accomplished, etc.	C
2. Methodology of costing out each activity in the WBS in terms of resources required and then aggregating the results	L
3. Dependences created by the nature of the project. Cannot be broken. They are referred to as *hard logic*	H
4. Precedence relationships between project activities that are within the team's control	O
5. The approved and accepted Scope Statement, WBS, and WBS Dictionary completed during project scope planning	A
6. Defines total project resource requirements using the WBS as a guide, and allows you to determine needs, gaps, issues, risks, etc.	M
7. A common method of developing a Project Network Diagram. Also referred to as AON methodology	F
8. The process of breaking down the Scope Statement into smaller and more manageable parts through creation of a WBS and WBS Dictionary	B
9. The process of beginning a successor activity prior to completion of the predecessor	J
10. Critical document used as an input for ALL schedule planning processes. Prescribes processes required to develop the end-to-end schedule	E
11. Established based on best practices. They are referred to as *soft or preferred logic*. The primary focus is to reduce risk	K
12. Documents identified risks potentially impacting a project. Identification begins with the Project Charter and doesn't end until all project planning is complete	I
13. A document that includes the most detailed version of project scope and drives project activity design efforts	D
14. Acknowledge non-project related activities that impact project activities outside control of the team. Often stem from regulations or standards	N
15. Successor activity cannot begin until the predecessor activity has begun. A key dependency relationship	G

Activity 3B: Schedule Model Creation Steps 5 - 8

Schedule Planning and Development (Steps 5 - 8)	Response
1. Involves using resources from non-critical path activities and applying them to critical path activities. Often increases costs	E
2. Uses WBS as a guide. Each Work Package is individually estimated for time durations and costs. Best used for complex and ambiguous projects where there are many unknowns	H
3. Techniques used to adjust project resources to meet resource constraints, limited availability, or project changes	F
4. Delays the start of the successor activity even though the predecessor activity may be complete	A
5. Weighted estimation model based on norms that state the Optimistic and Pessimistic results occur approximately one out of every six times, and the Most Likely result occurs approximately four out of six times	G
6. Most frequently used schedule presentation type for management presentations	P
7. Reserves that address times when project risks cannot be identified until planning progresses, or even project execution begins	I
8. Meeting that presents a proposed project schedule to stakeholders for review and acceptance. Occurs after Sponsor approval	S
9. Reserves that address risks identified on the Risk Register. Addresses known unknowns	O
10. Project activities are designated to support other work activities or the entire project. Often referred to as "Hammock Activities"	K
11. Tool that generates the schedule model. This tool and technique is the use of any and all tools to create and execute a schedule model successfully	R
12. Technique uses actual durations of previous, similarly scheduled activities or entire projects as a basis for time estimates. Most reliable when past projects are similar in fact and not just appearance	B
13. Adjust start and finish dates to balance demand for resources with supply. Often causes the original critical path to change, usually to increase	N

14. Eliminates dependencies for two activities planned to be completed sequentially. Can only be accomplished for dependencies that are not mandatory	T
15. Uses computer models, estimates of risk--expressed as probability distributions of both costs and durations, and typically uses a tool called Monte Carlo	M
16. Estimation uses three distinct estimates. Determine an Optimistic estimate, Most-Likely Estimate, and Pessimistic Estimate and use mathematical models to determine the best estimate	L
17. Adjusts activities to ensure requirements for resources do not exceed certain pre-defined resource limits. Does not impact critical path. Resources are adjusted or delayed within their free or total float	Q
18. Initial Project Network Diagram does not include time durations. It simply shows the logical flow of all activities based on dependency determinations	C
19. Sums three estimates and uses the average to determine the final estimate. Also called a *Triangular Distribution*	J
20. Technique quantitatively multiplies the quantity of work to be performed × the productivity rate. Uses regression analysis and learning curve techniques	D

Activity 4A: EVM Practice Scenario

Scenario 1: Your project delivered 60% of all required deliverables. You planned to be 70% complete with the entire project at this time. You spent $50,000 of your total $100,000 BAC allocation.

Calculate EV, PV, and AC into dollar amounts.

EV	EV = 60% × $100,000 = $60,000
PV	PV = 70% × $100,000 = $70,000
AC	AC = $50,000

Scenario 2: A six month project has a PV of $40,000 every two months. What is the BAC for this project?

BAC	There are 3 two-month periods $40,000 × 3 = $120,000 *Always assume linear returns

Activity 4B: EVM Practice Scenarios

1. You planned to complete 60% of a $50,000 project by this time. You completed 70% of the project. Actual costs to this point are $35,000. Calculate SV, CV, SPI, CPI, and EAC.

2. SV is $200 and CV $ -200. Your EV is $3,000. Calculate PV and AC.

3. CPI is .8. AC is $2,500. Calculate EV.

4. SPI is .91. EV is $2,000. Calculate PV. Round to nearest hundred dollars.

5. EV is $1,000. AC is $900 and PV is $950. Calculate CPI and SPI.

6. EV is $20,000. AC is $30,000 and PV is $25,000. Calculate TCPI for this this project to achieve a BAC goal of $50,000.

Answers:

1.	PV=$30,000. EV = $35,000. AC = $35,000. • SV = EV – PV ($35,000 -$30,000 = $5,000) • CV = EV – AC ($35,000 - $35,000 = $0) • SPI = (EV/PV) ($35,000/$30,000 = 1.17) • CPI = (EV/AC) ($35,000/$35,000 = 1.00)
2.	• Calculate PV: PV = EV-SV ($3,000 - $200 = $2,800) • Calculate AC: AC = EV – CV ($3,000 – (-$200) = $3,200)
3.	• EV = CPI × AC (.8 × $2,500 = $2,000)
4.	• PV = EV/SPI ($2,000/.91) = $2,200 (Rounded)
5.	• CPI = EV/AC ($1,000/$900)= 1.11 • SPI = EV/PV ($1,000/$950) = 1.05
6.	PV=$25,000. EV = $20,000. AC = $30,000. • TCPI for BAC = (BAC - EV)/(BAC – AC) • ($50,000 - $20,000)/($50,000 - $30,000) = $30,000/$20,000 = 1.5

Activity 4C: Network Diagram Analysis

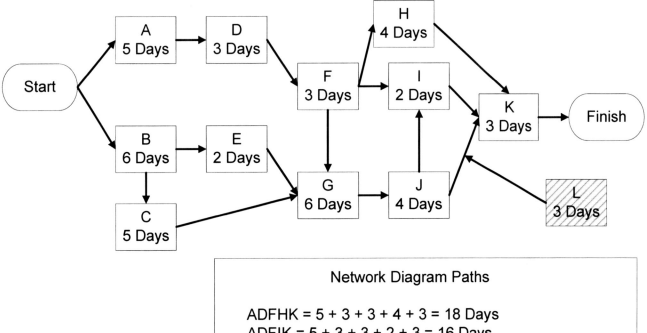

Network Diagram Paths

ADFHK = 5 + 3 + 3 + 4 + 3 = 18 Days
ADFIK = 5 + 3 + 3 + 2 + 3 = 16 Days
ADFGJK = 5 + 3 + 3 + 6 + 4 + 3 = 24 Days
BEGJK = 6 + 2 + 6 + 4 + 3 = 21 Days
BEGJIK = 6 + 2 + 6 + 4 + 2 + 3 = 23 Days
BCGJIK = 6 + 5 + 6 + 4 + 2 + 3 = 26 Days
BCGJK = 6 + 5 + 6 + 4 + 3 = 24 Days

Add Activity L: BCGJLK = 6 + 5 + 6 + 4 + 3 + 3 = 27 Days

What is critical path?	Path BCGJIK = 26 Days
Which activities have float?	Activities A, D, E, F, and H
A new Activity L is added between Activity J and K. Activity L is 3 Days. Impact?	New critical path is created. BCGJLK = 27 Days
After Activity L is added, what is "Near Critical Path"?	New "Near Critical Path" is BCGJIK = 26 Days
After Activity L is added, how much float does Activity I have if any?	Activity I no longer on critical path. Activity I has float of one day

Activity 4D: Schedule Monitoring and Controlling

Schedule Monitoring and Controlling Activity	Response
1. A dollar value tied to the estimated value of the work already accomplished on a project	F
2. Level of detail required to support a monthly report. Includes all major milestones, major project scheduling elements, and more	L
3. Defines working and non-working times for the project. Replaces the Project Calendar for actual schedule calculations	B
4. Metric that shows how the schedule is progressing according to the plan. You are behind schedule if this metric is less than 1.0	C
5. External group that reviews and approves/disapproves changes. Form if the project is large, or has a high-degree of competing stakeholder interests	I
6. Takes Work Performance Data and formats it to provide useable schedule performance information that can be used by stakeholders	D
7. *The #1 goal* of change management. Accomplish this goal by having a transparent change control system that is well communicated	N
8. Calculation that shows the level of effort required to complete a project based on BAC or EAC	A
9. One-page summary. Generally includes a high-level summary of activities and major contractual and project related milestones	J
10. Initially assigned to define working and non-working times for schedule activities and resources; i.e. holidays, weekend schedules, etc.	K
11. Industry standard used to measure planned versus actual schedule and cost performance. Provides current status snapshot of schedule and cost status	O
12. One of three methods used to calculate a project's *Activity Duration Percent Complete*	G
13. Share your findings with other project managers so they can take advantage of the knowledge gained over the course of a project	H
14. Compare planned versus actual project results, look for variations, and address them	E
15. Intended to ensure the project's standards are being followed and prevent potential problems from occurring	M

Activity 5: Schedule Closeout

Question	True or False
1. Verification of project deliverables occurs during the Validate Scope process	False. Verification of deliverables occurs in Control Quality.
2. Control Quality ensures the project conforms to requirements. Validate Scope ensures fit for use	True
3. Forensic Schedule Analysis may be used for legal proceedings and is performed retrospectively	True
4. Quality Audits analyzes the overall procurement process from planning to close to improve future project contractual performance	False. This is the Procurement Audit definition.
5. The customer is required to verify deliverables to determine if corrective changes are required	False. Customers accept deliverables during Validate Scope.
6. Settlement guidance shares how sellers and buyers can formally process and communicate contract issues	False. This is the Claims Administration definition.
7. Lessons Learned should be optimally conducted at the end of each phase	True
8. The Close Project or Phase process occurs once during every project	False. Process may occur on numerous occasions.
9. Lesson Learned sessions should always begin with a positive question	True
10. Work Authorization Systems are procedures that dictate how and when work can progress	True
11. The final step in the Closing process Group is to Close procurements	False. Final step is to Close Project or Phase.
12. The Schedule Management Plan should be archived for use by others in the future as part of Enterprise Environmental Factor updates	False. Included in Organizational Process Asset updates.

Activity 6: Stakeholder Communications Management

Stakeholder Communications Management Activity	Response
1. Documents current versus desired levels of stakeholder commitment and develops strategies.	H
2. Factors that may distort and interfere with understanding, transmission, or block the message.	L
3. Method of stakeholder classification that measures power, urgency, and legitimacy.	I
4. Process used to update stakeholder management strategies and address issues.	K
5. Primary method used to identify initial project stakeholders.	E
6. Defines who needs to receive schedule related communications to include information, responses, status, meetings, etc.	C
7. Document that identifies key stakeholders by role.	J
8. Responsible to encode the message and selects the proper medium to get it to the receiver.	G
9. Recommended method to manage a low power and high interest stakeholder.	B
10. Information available to stakeholders at their discretion; i.e. share point or web site.	A
11. Stakeholder who has yet to determine the level of support they are willing to a project.	F
12. Result of transforming Work Performance Data into a more useable format.	D

Activity 7A: PMBOK Chapter 1 through 4 Review

Question	True or False
1. All change requests should be listed on a master Issues Log that supports the project.	False. All change requests should be listed on a Change Control Log. Issues Logs are reserved for risks that became issues or questions needing answers.
2. The Monitoring and Controlling Process Group follows the Planning Process Group.	False. Monitoring and Controlling Process Group follows Executing Process Group.
3. Configuration Management focuses on controlling changes to the project's product or service's functional and physical characteristics.	True.
4. Team members may be obligated to report to two managers in a Matrix organizational model.	True.
5. The focus of the Functional organizational model is on projects.	False. Focus on projects is a characteristic of the Projectized organizational model.
6. "Silo" is a term often associated with the Matrix organizational model.	False. "Silo" is associated with the Functional organizational model.
7. Stakeholders are refusing to buy-in to overall project goals. In all likelihood, more time should have been spent on the Cultural and Social Environment.	True.
8. The PMI Framework consists of six interrelated Process Groups beginning with Initiating and ending with Closing.	False. There are five interrelated Process Groups.

Activity 7B: Project Quality and Human Resource Management Review

Question	True or False
1. A Theory X manager is one who believes people should be trusted and are self-directed.	False. This definition fits Theory Y manager.
2. David McClelland is responsible for developing the Achievement Motivation Theory.	True.
3. According to Hertzberg's Theory, salary is a hygiene factor and responsibility is a motivating agent.	True.
4. Maslow created the Hierarchy of Needs Theory which places Esteem on the top rung.	False. Maslow did create the theory. However, Self-Actualization is the top level.
5. Training and instructing others is an attribute of the Consensus Building leadership style.	False. This attribute matches the Coaching leadership style.
6. Autocratic leaders generally make decisions with little or no input from others.	True.
7. A team entered the Storming phase. Facilitative and Consensus Building leadership styles are optimal in this phase.	True.
8. Performing is normally a step that a team achieves prior to Norming.	False. Steps in the Tuckman model are Forming, Storming, Norming, Performing and Adjourning.
9. A Functional Manager is a stakeholder who authorizes the project manager.	False. Functional Managers provide human resources for the project.
10. Key metrics and performance objectives are defined in the Quality Management Plan.	True.
11. The primary tool used to accomplish Quality Assurance is inspections.	False. Primary tool to accomplish Quality Assurance is a Quality Audit.
12. Quality Checklists are developed for use in Control Quality and documented in the Quality Management Plan.	True.

Activity 7C: Project Risk Management

Risk Management Definition and Concept Activity	Response
1. Provides reserves to support risk identified on the Risk Register	H
2. The primary focus of Quantify Risks	L
3. Risks that may result directly from implementing a planned Contingency Plan	E
4. A document that defines methods a project will employ to manage risk	J
5. May be required to request additional reserves for a newly identified risk response	F
6. A risk response that enlists the support of third parties to achieve an opportunity	A
7. Risks that remain after implementing a planned Risk Response Plan. They must be accounted for on the Risk Register	D
8. Lists risk categories and sub-categories in hierarchical order to help identify risks	N
9. A process that identifies new risks, reassesses current risks, and closes out risks that are no longer applicable	C
10. Tool that calculates risk contingency requirements by multiplying the probability of a risk times its potential dollar impact	M
11. A risk response that aims to reduce the probability and/or the impact of a threat	P
12. The primary focus of Qualify Risks	K
13. The product of risk probability times risk impact	O
14. Examines and documents the effectiveness of risk responses and the overall Risk Management Process	B
15. A document used to document project risks throughout the duration of the project	G
16. Compares project technical accomplishments to the schedule defining when technical achievement is required	I

Activity 7D: Project Procurement Management

Question/Statement	Response
1. There are _____ steps in the end-to-end Project Procurement Process	4
2. The procurement _____ should provide enough information for a seller to submit a proposal	SOW
3. Source selection criteria should be applied _____ to all seller proposals	Equally
4. Justification why internal resources cannot meet project schedule needs are include in the _____	Make or Buy Decision
5. A _____ contract outlines specific deliverable requirements places risk on the seller	Fixed Price
6. A _____ contract is used when you are buying expertise you need to complete a deliverable	Cost Reimbursement
7. A _____ contract would be used for a quick requirement that is not overly technical	Time and Material
8. Three types of procurement documents are an IFB, RFP, and _____	RFQ
9. Procurement settlements occur during the _____ process of project procurement management	Close Procurements
10. Generally, changes to a procurement contract are processed through a _____	Contract Control System

APPENDIX B: 150-Question Test

Congratulations on completing all activities. Here is a challenging 150-question test representative of questions on the PMI-SP Certification Exam.

Read questions and answers carefully. Answers with explanations are provided at the end of the test. Try to achieve 75% or approximately 112 questions correct. Take the test again and again until you can reach and achieve this goal or higher.

Question #	Question	Responses	Response
1.	A Project Scheduler is looking for an automated application that helps perform schedule network analysis. What should they use?	a. Presentations b. Instances c. Scheduling tool d. Schedule model	
2.	You are analyzing reserve requirements for your project. You want to identify reserves for unknown risks you suspect will materialize by the end of the project. What type of reserves is needed?	a. Contingency Reserves b. Expected Monetary Value c. Management Reserves d. Discretionary Reserves	
3.	You are ready to sequence activities to continue creation of the schedule model. What must be completed prior to beginning this step?	a. Define Milestones b. Determine Durations c. Determine Resources d. Approve the Schedule	
4.	How far should an activity be broken down during the Design Project Activities step?	a. No more than twice the reporting cycle b. Less than half of the reporting cycle c. No longer than the reporting cycle d. Less than one fourth of the reporting cycle	

5.	Which of the following is not a traditional type of buffer used to implement Critical Chain Method?	a. Resource Buffer b. Delay Buffer ⭕ c. Project Buffer d. Feeding Buffer	
6.	The Project Scheduler must be aware of where potential team members work, and develop relationships with Functional Managers managing resources you need on the project. What tool will help most?	a. WBS b. RBS c. OBS ⭕ d. PMB	
7.	A project manager normally spends what percentage of their time communicating?	a. 75% b. 82% c. 90% ⭕ d. 95%	
8.	You are using specific outputs from the schedule model to communicate data for analysis and decision making. What are these outputs?	a. Presentations ⭕ b. Instances c. Schedule network analysis d. Scheduling Reports	
9.	Agile project management uses what form of scheduling methodology?	a. AOA b. ADM c. Critical Chain Method d. CPM ⭕	
10.	A Project Scheduler is anxious to create a schedule model to support a project. What step must be completed prior to schedule model creation?	a. Generate presentations b. Determine scheduling tool ⭕ c. Generate instances d. Review network diagram	
11.	Your team is established and working well together. For the most part, they know the work to be done and remain focused. Which leadership style is best suited for this team?	a. Coaching b. Supportive ⭕ c. Facilitative d. Autocratic	

12.	The most common approach to implementing CPM that provides a network diagram showing all required activities and durations is:	a. PDM b. ADM c. AOA d. Agile	
13.	A Project Scheduler is managing a project with many unknowns. She elects to use a method that provides detailed plans for known activities, and develops planning packages for less defined activities. What method is being used?	a. Rolling Wave Planning b. Critical Chain Method c. Agile d. ADM	
14.	Risk is best defined as:	a. An uncertain event that can impact the project negatively b. An uncertain event that can impact at least one project objective c. An unknown event that can impact project objectives d. An uncertain event that occurs during Project Executing	
15.	You are trying to determine the difference between Adaptive and Predictive project management systems. What is true regarding Adaptive systems?	a. Uses numerous buffers to account for risk b. Develops User Stories which are used to complete a Scope Statement c. Uses a WBS and WBS Dictionary to define activities d. Uses a Product Backlog to define requirements	
16.	A project team member needs to access information regarding scheduling methods, schedule tools, and schedule configuration management procedures. What is the best source?	a. Performance Management Baseline b. Project Charter c. Schedule Management Plan d. Schedule Baseline	

17.	Which are the top two sources of power for a project manager?	a. Reward/Referent b. Expert/Formal c. Reward/Expert d. Formal/Referent	
18.	Acknowledging the organization's structure, systems, and culture to include standards and regulations impacting your project are accomplished by analysis of:	a. Organizational Process Assets b. Enterprise Environmental Factors c. WBS Dictionary d. Productivity Index Charts	
19.	Completing a car assembly before it can be removed from an assembly line is an example of:	a. Start-to-Start b. Finish-to-Finish c. Start-to-Finish d. Finish-to-Start	
20.	A Project Scheduler analyzed schedule outputs and noted an activity lacking a predecessor. How is this activity referred to?	a. Incomplete b. Out of Scope c. Critical Path d. Open Ended	
21.	ADM can only use which relationship?	a. Start-to-Start b. Finish-to-Finish c. Start-to-Finish d. Finish-to-Start	
22.	A Project Scheduler identified an activity that can begin before the predecessor activity is 100% complete. What is she considering?	a. Lead b. Lag c. Resource Leveling d. Resource Smoothing	
23.	There are a total of eight stakeholders a project. How many total communications channels exist?	a. 8 b. 28 c. 36 d. 56	
24.	Key events or points in time that must be met to achieve project goals and objectives are identified during which step of the Schedule Model Creation process?	a. Determine Resources b. Design Project Activities c. Determine Durations d. Define Milestones	

25.	The sequence activities step is complete. All of the following can be analyzed except:	a. Network Logic b. Critical Path c. Activity Dependencies d. Path Convergence	
26.	You are managing a project with five Work Packages. Two Work Packages are complete, two are started, and one has not started. You are using a 50/50 progress reporting method. What is the percent complete?	a. 40% b. 60% c. 80% d. 100%	
27.	A scheduler is preparing a project schedule status presentation for management. What is the optimal presentation method?	a. Bar Chart b. Milestone Chart c. Project Network Diagram d. Variance Chart	
28.	Activity C is scheduled to complete on Day 19. It is now Day 22 and Activity C is not started. Which statement is true?	a. Free float is 3 b. Negative float is -3 c. Total float is 3 d. LOE activity is required	
29.	Project BAC is $5,000. EV is $3,000, PV is $2,500, and AC is $3,500. What is the TCPI to achieve BAC?	a. 1.66 b. .75 c. 1.33 d. .6 _TCPI = (5k - 3w) / (5k - 3.5w)_	
30.	Using one-point estimation is correct what percentage of the time?	a. 10% b. 15% c. 25% d. 50%	
31.	All of the following inputs are essential to sequence activities except:	a. Activity Attributes b. Milestones c. Activity List d. RBS	
32.	Pierre needs to solicit ideas from experts located in multiple geographic areas. He plans to use a questionnaire to collect feedback. Which information gathering technique is this?	a. Root Cause Analysis b. Sensitivity Analysis c. Delphi Technique d. Nominal Group Technique	

33.	The optimal scheduling estimation method to use when there is complexity and ambiguity is:	a. Analogous b. Expert (c.) Bottom Up d. Parametric	
34.	A Project Scheduler identified a dependency within the team's control to manage. This dependency is best defined as:	a. Mandatory b. Discretionary c. External (d.) Internal	
35.	A Project Scheduler was notified project deliverables are complete. What is the first step that must be taken in the closure process?	a. Control Quality b. Validate Scope c. Close Procurements d. Transition Product	
36.	You want to implement a system requiring certain criteria to be met prior to proceeding to each successor activity. What should you consider?	a. EVM (b.) Work Authorization System c. Process Directives d. Performance Measurement Plan	
37.	What key output would you refer to determine the greatest potential for path convergence?	a. WBS b. WBS Dictionary c. Activity Duration Estimates d. Project Network Diagram	
38.	The most detailed document defining scope driving schedule planning is?	a. WBS b. Scope Statement c. WBS Dictionary d. Scope Management Plan	
39.	Activity A is valued at $2,000 and 80% complete. Activity B is valued at $3,000 and 40% complete. Activity C is valued at $5,000 and 100% complete. What is EV?	a. $7,800 b. $10,000 c. $5,000 d. $0	

<table>
<tr><td>40.</td><td>A Project Scheduler produced three-schedule iterations based on risk. The optimistic schedule is 6 days, most likely is 11 days, and pessimistic 22 days. What is the time estimate using a beta distribution method?</td><td>a. 13 Days
b. 39 Days
c. 12 Days
d. 19.5 Days</td><td></td></tr>
<tr><td>41.</td><td>You are managing a complex project that introduces new deliverables and processes to the organization. There are a number of ambiguities to be addressed as potential risks. Which estimating method serves this project best?</td><td>a. Analogous
b. Bottom Up
c. Parametric
d. Expert</td><td></td></tr>
<tr><td>42.</td><td>You are planning a project with 9 stakeholders and you. How many communications channels exist?</td><td>a. 10
b. 36
c. 45
d. 20</td><td></td></tr>
<tr><td>43.</td><td>A key stakeholder currently agrees with a project's concept but is not actively engaged. How would this stakeholder be best classified?</td><td>a. Neutral
b. Supportive
c. Leading
d. Committed</td><td></td></tr>
<tr><td>44.</td><td>Calculate critical path using this table:
<table>
<tr><th>Activity</th><th>Preceding Activity</th><th>Duration in Days</th></tr>
<tr><td>Start</td><td></td><td>0</td></tr>
<tr><td>A</td><td>Start</td><td>3</td></tr>
<tr><td>B</td><td>Start</td><td>2</td></tr>
<tr><td>C</td><td>Start</td><td>6</td></tr>
<tr><td>D</td><td>A, F</td><td>5</td></tr>
<tr><td>E</td><td>D, G</td><td>4</td></tr>
<tr><td>F</td><td>B</td><td>3</td></tr>
<tr><td>G</td><td>C</td><td>3</td></tr>
<tr><td>Finish</td><td>E</td><td>0</td></tr>
</table></td><td>a. 12 Days
b. 13 Days
c. 14 Days
d. 15 Days</td><td></td></tr>
</table>

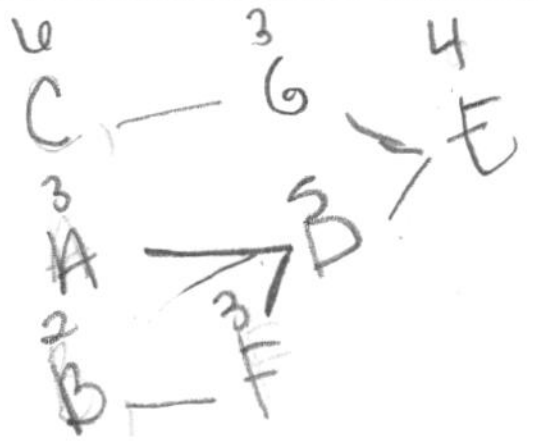

Use the following scenario to respond to questions 45 through 47.

You are managing a four-month project with BAC of $80,000. You are two months into the project and planned to have 50% completed. The EV is 40%, and you used $45,000 of the allotted budget.

45.	What is current SPI?	a. 1.41 b. .71 c. .8 ⊙ d. 1.25	32k/40k
46.	What is SV?	a. ($8,000) ⊙ b. $8,000 c. ($13,000) d. $13,000	32-40
47.	What strategy is (not) viable? SPI>1 CPI<1	a. Fast Track b. Change Network Logic c. Perform Value Analysis d. Crash	
48.	You identified two risks. There is a 30% Risk A will cost $2,000. There is a 60% chance Risk B will cost $8,000. What is the EMV?	a. $10,000 b. $6.000 c. $5,400 ⊙ d. $0	
49.	You use a weighted estimation method. The pessimistic estimate is 33 days, most likely estimate 25 days, and optimistic estimate 11 days. What is the estimate for duration?	a. 24 Days ⊙ b. 23 Days c. 25 Days d. 33 Days	33+100+11
50.	The Sponsor was unhappy with resource tasking and wants to balance out working times to make them more linear. The affected activities are on critical path. What tool should be implemented?	a. Resource Smoothing b. Resource Levelling ⊙ c. Fast Tracking d. Simulation	

51.	Which statement regarding Lessons Learned is most correct?	a. Best conducted at the closure of the project. b. Aid in refining risk policies and practices. c. Always conducted formally to assist future project managers. d. Address past and future situations that likely impact future projects.	
52.	A Project Scheduler wants to determine who to share status and required reports with. What is the best source?	a. Schedule Management Plan b. Communications Management Plan c. Project Scope Statement d. RBS	
53.	A Project Scheduler is using a tool that provides probabilities of completing schedule and/or time objectives. What is this tool and when is it used?	a. Monte Carlo/Simulation b. Monte Carlo/Compression Techniques c. PERT/Simulation d. PERT/Compression Techniques	
54.	The Project Management Plan is approved and ready for stakeholder acceptance. What meeting should be scheduled to attain acceptance?	a. Sponsor One on One b. Pre-Baseline Presentation c. Kick Off Meet d. Customer Acceptance Meet	
55.	Which of the following processes use inspections to determine results?	a. Quality Assurance/Validate Scope b. Control Quality/Control Scope c. Quality Assurance/Control Scope d. Control Quality/Validate Scope	
56.	A project team verified deliverables met all specifications. What next step must be taken before closing out the project phase?	a. Close Procurements b. Control Quality c. Validate Scope d. Transition Product	

57.	You have three estimates to complete a project activity. The pessimistic estimate is 25 days. Most likely is 16 days and optimistic is 10 days. How much time should you plan for the activity?	a. 15 Days b. 16 Days c. 17 Days d. 19 Days	
58.	Communications blockers are impacting project communications. What likely results?	a. Paralingual communications b. Urgency of need c. Less ease of use d. Conflict	
59.	A project manager is using e-mail to discuss team issues. This is classified as what type of communication?	a. Formal Written b. Informal Written c. Pull Communications d. Push Communications	
60.	You completed a brainstorming session and identified multiple stakeholders. What method is best to identify additional stakeholders beyond the initial list?	a. Interview b. Delphi Technique c. Nominal Group Technique d. SWOT	

Figure T.1 Questions 60 - 65

Refer to the Figure below for questions 60 – 65. Duration is days.

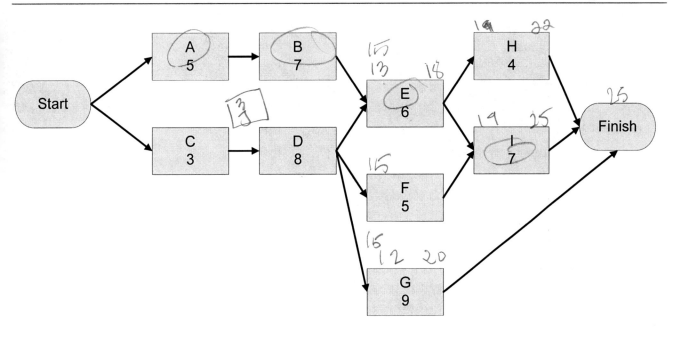

61.	What is critical path?	a. 23 b. 25 c. 21 d. 22	
62.	Which activity has float?	a. A b. E c. I d. H	
63.	A new activity of 3 days (Activity J) is placed between Activity C and D. What is the impact?	a. Activity J has float b. New Critical Path is created c. Critical Path is unchanged d. Activity G on critical path	
64.	Once Activity J is added, which is "Near Critical Path"?	a. CJDFI b. CJDH c. ABEI d. ABEH	
65.	Activity A and B are fast tracked. What is the duration of path ABEI?	a. 25 Days b. 18 Days c. 20 Days d. 17 Days	

66.	Which of the following would not be classified as a technology factor impacting effective communications?	a. Ease of Use b. Project Environment c. Push Communications d. Urgency of need for information
67.	A project manager reviewed a Stakeholder Register as part of her duties. During which Process Group is the Stakeholder Register developed?	a. Initiating b. Planning c. Executing d. Monitoring and Controlling
68.	You want to use a group creativity technique that uses brainstorming and a voting process to rank order ideas. Which technique is best?	a. Root Cause Analysis b. Sensitivity Analysis c. Delphi Technique d. Nominal Group Technique
69.	A team sequenced activities for a critical IT project valued at $200,000. They defined a precedence relationship between project activities within the team's control, but still needs to be documented and considered. How would you classify this dependency?	a. External b. Mandatory c. Discretionary d. Internal
70.	You used a beta distribution method to estimate project costs. Which formula is most appropriate?	a. (P +4ML + O)/6 b. (P +ML + O)/3 c. (P-O)/6 d. (P+O)/6
71.	Which tools and techniques are considered Resource Optimization methods?	a. Resource Leveling/Leads b. Resource Smoothing/Resource Leveling c. Resource Smoothing/Lags d. Leads/Lags

Figure T.2 Questions 72-77

Use the information in this table for questions 72 – 77.

$CPI = .909$

Activity	% Complete	Value	Actual Costs	EV
A	100%	$2,000	$2,000	2000
B	70%	$4,000	$3,000	2800
C	40%	$3,000	$1,400	1200
D	0%	$2,000	$200	0
E	0%	$4,000	$0	0
Project Planned to be 50% complete at this time				6000

72.	What is EV?	a. $9,000 b. $6,400 c. $6,000 d. $15,000	
73.	What is BAC?	a. $9,000 b. $6,400 c. $6,000 d. $15,000	
74.	Calculate SPI? $\frac{6k}{7500}$	a. .91 b. .80 c. ($1,500) d. ($600)	
75.	What is true?	a. SPI is greater than 1.0 b. Project is ahead of schedule c. SPI is less than 1.0 d. Project is under budget	
76.	What measure cannot be taken?	a. Fast Track b. Crash c. Change Logic d. What-If Scenario Analysis	

77.	If nothing changes, what is project EAC?	a. $16,500 b. $15,000 c. $6,800 d. 100%	
78.	A Schedule Planner is trying to determine the best way to determine how schedule issues should be communicated and to whom. What is the optimal tool?	a. Stakeholder Register b. Risk Register c. Work Performance Report d. Communications Management Plan	

Figure T.3 Questions 79-82

Use the Figure below for questions 79 – 82. Duration is days.

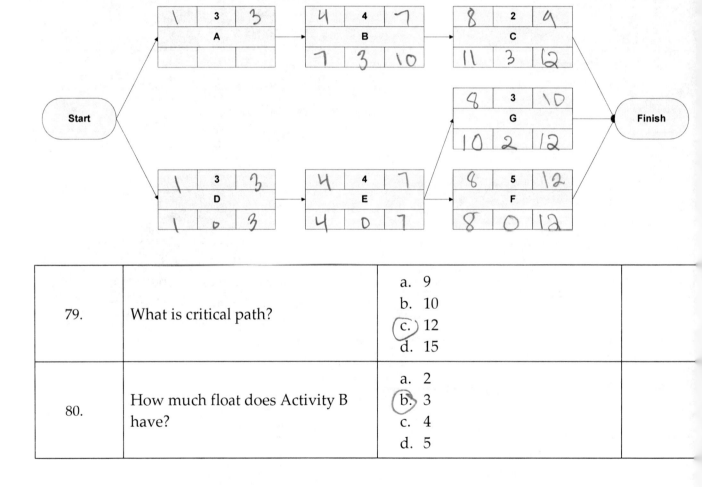

79.	What is critical path?	a. 9 b. 10 c. 12 d. 15	
80.	How much float does Activity B have?	a. 2 b. 3 c. 4 d. 5	

81.	What is LS for Activity G?	a. 12 b. 11 c. 9 (d.) 10	
82.	What is EF for Activity C?	a. 7 (b.) 9 c. 11 d. 12	
83.	A project team is in the storming stage of development. Which leadership style is least effective at this point?	a. Facilitative (b.) Autocratic c. Consensus Building (d.) Consultative	
84.	Which is the greatest source for potential conflict in a project?	a. Budget b. Personalities c. Leadership Styles (d.) Schedules	
85.	A project team analyzed the overall procurement process from planning to close to determine how future contractual performance can be improved. What activity occurred?	a. Forensic Analysis (b.) Procurement Audit c. Quality Audit d. Claims Administration	
86.	What is true regarding this activity (Use days for estimates)? | 8	6	13
F
10	2	15		(a.) Float is 2 days b. Early start is Day 10 c. Activity is on Critical Path d. Early finish is Day 15	

87.	You collected raw observations and measurements impacting all facets of a business application development project. What is the next step?	a. Share data with the Project Sponsor b. Develop Work Performance Reports c. Create Work Performance Information d. Request additional Work Performance Data	
88.	You reviewed performance reports and determined PV is $2,000, EV is $2,200, and AC is $1,800. Which statement is true?	a. CV is $ -400 b. SV is $ -200 c. CPI is 1.22 d. SPI is 1.22	
89.	You determined a Work Package on critical path has negative float. What possible action should not be taken?	a. Change schedule logic b. Fast track c. Crash d. Let customer know the schedule will change	
90.	A numbering system used to identify each component of a WBS and determine the level of the node or activity is called a:	a. Code of Account Identifier b. Chart of Account Identifier c. WBS Dictionary d. Work Package	
91.	Nicole is using an estimation technique that uses estimates from prior projects similar to hers. What estimating technique is she using?	a. Parametric b. Analogous c. Three Point d. Bottom Up	

Figure T.4 Questions 92-95

Refer to the figure below for questions 92 – 95. Durations is days.

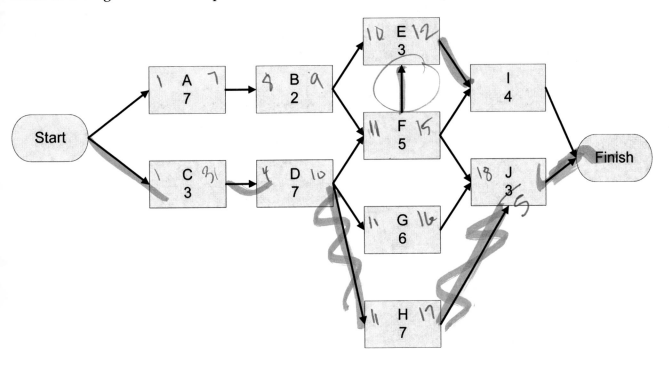

92.	What is critical path?	a. 19 Days b. 20 Days c. 21 Days d. 22 Days	
93.	Which is Near Critical Path?	a. CDFI b. CDFEI c. ABFEI d. CDHJ	
94.	Which activity has float?	a. A b. F c. E d. I	
95.	Activity J is extended 2 days. How many critical paths exist?	a. 1 b. 2 c. 3 d. 4	

96.	You want to identify key customers to ensure they are interviewed and participate in the Schedule Planning Process. Which input will provide you with this information?	a. Stakeholder Register b. Stakeholder Management Strategy c. Communications Management Plan d. Lessons Learned	
97.	Which of the following risk strategies are best when you require external resources to achieve an opportunity or reduce a threat?	a. Share/Mitigate b. Transfer/Enhance c. Share/Transfer d. Mitigate/Enhance	
98.	You developed an SOW for a fixed price contract. Which is the optimal procurement document to use?	a. RFQ b. IFB c. RFP d. MB	
99.	Three point estimating is a tool that provides us a:	a. Triangular or Alpha Distribution b. Alpha or Beta Distribution c. Alpha or Omega Distribution d. Triangular or Beta Distribution	
100.	You defined a dependency to reduce risk now being analyzed for elimination to compress schedules. Which dependency type is this?	a. Mandatory b. Discretionary c. External d. Internal	
101.	Issue Logs help identify and address questions the team or others may have about the project, along with addressing risks that occurred. When are issues logs generated?	a. Identify Stakeholders b. Plan Stakeholder Management c. Control Stakeholder Engagement d. Manage Stakeholder Engagement	
102.	The most common network diagramming network method is referred to as:	a. GERT b. AON c. ADM d. AOA	

103.	You reviewed activity resource requirements to develop a project schedule. You used CPM, but suspect there may be resource constraints that reduce chances of success. You added buffers to prevent uncertainties. What tool and technique did you use?	a. Schedule Compression b. Resource Leveling c. Critical Chain Method d. Schedule network analysis	
104.	A Project Scheduler has been asked to provide cause and effect analysis of a project to be used in legal proceedings. What activity is called for?	a. Forensic Schedule Analysis b. Procurement Audit c. Quality Audit d. Claims Administration	
105.	A project manager wants to develop a contract posing the least amount of Cost Risk to the buyer. Which contract best suits this purpose?	a. Firm Fixed Price b. Time and Material c. Cost Plus Percentage of Cost d. Request for Quote	
106.	Project BAC is $60,000. As of today, project is 40% complete. This is better than the 30% planned completion level forecast for this point in the project. A total of $25,000 has been expended for the project. Which statement is true?	a. Project is behind schedule b. Project is ahead on budget c. Schedule Variance is negative d. Cost Variance is negative	
107.	Using the information in question 106, what is the project's current SPI?	a. .96 b. 1.33 c. -$1,000 d. $6,000	
108.	A project manager created an issues log and is currently implementing strategy to change Resistor's opinions of the project. Which process is being accomplished?	a. Identify Stakeholders b. Plan Stakeholder Management c. Manage Stakeholder Engagement d. Control Stakeholder Engagement	

109.	There are communications technology factors impacting project communications. Which is not considered a communications technology factor during project planning?	a. Ease of use ✓ b. Sensitivity and Confidentiality of Information ✓ c. Project Environment ✓ d. Organizational Structure	
110.	A team is performing extensive market research in response to a need for third-party resource support. What process is the team engaged in?	a. Close Procurements b. Control Procurements c. Conduct Procurements d. Plan Procurement Management	
111.	You completed the project schedule and noted a few dependencies that could be fast tracked if needed. These dependencies are classified as:	a. Soft or preferred logic b. Hard logic c. Non project related dependencies d. Mandatory and Discretionary dependencies	
112.	You have solid time data per unit for your project along with defined quantities. Which estimation method is optimal?	a. Expert b. Parametric c. Bottom Up d. Analogous	
113.	You are managing a road pavement project. This four week project paves 20 miles of road at five miles per week. The estimated BAC is $100,000. You completed week two of the project and AC is $56,000. EV is $48,000. What is PV?	a. $50,000 b. ($8,000) c. $52,000 d. $44,000	
114.	You completed a review of a project. The SPI is .93 and CPI is 1.07. What should you consider?	a. Crashing to improve schedule performance b. Crashing to improve budget performance c. Fast tracking to improve schedule performance d. Fast tracking to improve budget performance	

115.	What is the most likely result of communications blockers?	a. Schedule delays b. Conflict c. Cost overruns d. Information delays	
116.	There are hygiene factors and motivating agents. Hygiene factors such as salary, working conditions, benefits, etc. can only destroy motivation. They do not increase motivation. Motivating factors such as responsibility, growth, and achievement are those that increase motivation. Who is responsible for this theory?	a. Maslow b. McClelland c. McGregor d. Hertzberg	
117.	You completed a backward pass for a project. Which statement is true?	a. Shows early start and early finish dates b. Calculates early and late starts and early and late finish dates c. Shows early start and late start dates d. Shows late start and late finish dates	
118.	You received a critical change request from a high-level stakeholder who wants it implemented immediately. What is your next step?	a. Log and evaluate the impact of the change immediately b. Call an emergency team meeting and make the change c. Contact the sponsor and gain approval to move forward d. Explain to the stakeholder that it is not practical to change the project after baseline	

119.	Stakeholders cannot agree on key scope issues driving schedule development. Who should normally be given primary consideration when disputes develop?	a. Team b. Project Champion c. Project Manager d. Customer	~
120.	A stakeholder manages using a "hands off" style. Which leadership type best describes this manager?	a. Facilitative b. Consultative c. Participative d. Laissez-Faire	
121.	A Project Scheduler is trying to determine how project standards will be adhered to and key metrics driving performance. What is the best source?	a. Schedule Management Plan b. Scope Statement c. Quality Management Plan d. Scope Management Plan	
122.	You completed a brainstorming session with stakeholders. You did not attain information you required. What action may have impacted effectiveness of this session?	a. Evaluated all ideas b. Used sticky notes c. Requested experts to attend d. Took time to log all inputs	
123.	You are using a Supporting Leadership Style to manage your team. Which stages of team development is best suited to this leadership style?	a. Forming and Storming b. Norming and Performing c. Forming and Norming d. Performing and Storming	
124.	You are dealing with a High Power and Low Interest stakeholder. What is the best strategy?	a. Keep Satisfied b. Monitor c. Manage Closely d. Keep Informed	
125.	You need critical input from experts to plan a controversial IT project. You plan to use a tool and technique which reduces fear of reprisal. You will consolidate all inputs and provide a final report to all who contribute. Which tool and technique are you using?	a. Nominal Group Technique b. Interviews c. Sensitivity Analysis d. Delphi Technique	

126.	A Project Scheduler reports directly to a project manager with high levels of authority and independence. What is the organizational structure?	a. Functional b. Weak Matrix c. Projectized d. Strong Matrix	
127.	Stakeholders are unhappy about a process change process and pushing back. Which environment should have been better addressed?	a. Cultural and Social b. Political c. Physical d. Configuration Management	
128.	You are using the Salience model to classify stakeholders. What is not a consideration for classification?	a. Power b. Influence c. Urgency d. Legitimacy	

Figure T.5 Questions 129-131

Use the chart for questions 129, 130, and 131. This chart supports a 10 Day activity.

Team Member	A	B	C
Skill/Efficiency Level	.8	1	.75
Availability	100%	60%	80%

129.	How long will it take to complete this activity if Team Members A, B and C all work together?	a. 10 Days b. 8 Days c. 5 Days d. 3 Days	
130.	How long will it take to complete this activity if Team Member A is the only resource?	a. 10 Days b. 12.5 Days c. 8 Days d. 11 Days	
131.	What is Team Member C's Productivity Index?	a. .6 b. .75 c. .8 d. 1.55	

207

132.	Ben plans to use a tool to consolidate ideas through individual brainstorming sessions into a single map to reflect commonality and differences in understanding, and generate new ideas. What is this tool?	a. Ishikawa Diagram b. Pareto Chart c. Idea/Mind Map d. Affinity Diagram	
133.	You reviewed desired commitment levels for key stakeholders and determined strategies to gain buy-in for schedule related activities were not yielding results. You adjusted current strategies to gain support you need. What process are you performing?	a. Identify Stakeholders b. Control Stakeholder Engagement c. Manage Stakeholder Engagement d. Plan Stakeholder Management	
134.	A project team plans to use Monte Carlo to determine the probability of meeting certain project time and cost goals. What tool and technique does Monte Carlo support?	a. Critical Chain Method b. Crashing c. Simulation d. Resource Smoothing	
135.	Which of the following conditions would not likely result from an open ended activity?	a. False picture of potential float b. Reduced potential to identify risk c. Obscure logical relationships d. Improper duration estimate	
136.	A project manager is using What-If scenarios to calculate potential results. She believes this modeling technique helps determine which risks have the greatest impact on a project. What tool is being used?	a. Sensitivity Analysis b. FMEA c. Delphi Technique d. Nominal Group Technique	
137.	Which of the following entries would not likely be documented in a Communications Management Plan?	a. Glossary b. Communications Model c. Integrated Change Control d. Constraints	

138.	You are expecting a number of issues with an upcoming contract impacting project deliverables. What should you consider?	a. Forensic Schedule Analysis b. Procurement Audit c. Claims Administration d. Negotiated Settlement	
139.	Project BAC is $4,000. PV is $2,200 and AC is $1,800. Project is 50% complete. What is the best strategy?	a. Crash b. Perform Value Analysis c. Fast Track d. Change Network Logic	
140.	You need to develop a document that lists strategies to move stakeholders from current to desired commitment levels. What document is best?	a. Stakeholder Management Plan b. RACI c. Stakeholder Register d. Human Resource Plan	
141.	EV is $2,500. PV is $3,000 and AC is $2,250. Which statement is true? $SPI = <1$ $CPI = >1$	a. Project is ahead of schedule b. Project is over budget c. SV is positive d. CV is positive	
142.	You determined that your SV is ($2,000). Your EV is $12,000. What is the PV at this point?	a. ($10,000) b. $2,000 c. $14,000 d. $10,000	

Figure T.6 Questions 143-144

$$(SV) = 12k - PV$$
$$-2k + 2 + PV$$
$$PV \qquad \frac{+2 + PV}{14}$$

4	2	5
	B	
6	2	7

Use this figure to answer questions 143 and 144

143.	Which statement is accurate?	a. Activity is on critical path b. Duration is 1 day c. Activity is behind schedule d. Float is 2 days	

144.	What is the LF?	a. 4 Days b. 5 Days c. 6 Days (d.) 7 Days	
145.	You need to determine project activities and Work Packages to better define project scheduling needs. Which document can best support your needs?	a. Scope Statement b. WBS c. Schedule Management Plan d. Schedule model	
146.	You need a document that defines working and non-working times for the project that can be used for actual schedule calculations. Which is the best option?	a. Activity Calendar b. RBS c. Resource Calendar d. Organizational Process Assets	
147.	Raj needs to pinpoint a specific Work Package in the WBS to determine if buffers are required. Each Work Package can be identified by:	a. WBS Numeric Designator b. Code of Account Identifier c. Work Package Code d. Chart of Account Identifier	
148.	The primary goal of an effective Integrated Change Control system is to:	a. Process change promptly b. Approve all changes c. Influence factors causing change d. Evaluate and prioritize all changes	
149.	You need to submit a monthly report that includes all milestones and major scheduling elements. Which format is optimal?	a. Level 2: Management Summary b. Level 3: Publication Schedule c. Level 4: Execution Planning d. Level 5: Detailed Planning	
150.	A project manager plans to apply resources from an activity with float to an activity on critical path that is challenged. What is not occurring?	a. Compression Techniques b. Risk of Increased Costs c. Risk of Near Critical Path creation d. Resource Optimization Techniques	

Final Test Solutions and Explanations

Question #	Response	Rationale
1.	C	Scheduling tools are automated applications that helps perform schedule network analysis.
2.	C	Management reserves are used to provide contingency for unknown risks or unknown unknowns.
3.	A	In the Schedule Model Creation Process, Define Milestones, then Define Activities prior to Sequencing Activities.
4.	B	A normal rule of thumb is any given activity should be broken down to complete in a timeframe less than half of the normal reporting cycle.
5.	B	Buffer designations in Critical Chain Method include project buffers, feeding buffers, and resource buffers.
6.	C	OBS is a hierarchical organizational chart depicting the top-down organizational model for the firm.
7.	C	Project managers spend approximately 90% of time communicating.
8.	A	Presentations are specific outputs from the schedule model to communicate key data used for analysis and decision making.
9.	D	Agile uses a form of CPM to develop schedules.
10.	B	Create schedule model is step 3 in the project scheduling process. Determine the scheduling method, then the scheduling tool before creating the schedule model.
11.	B	Team is most likely in the norming stage. Supporting leadership style is best suited. Coaching is best when team is forming. Facilitative is best during storming. Autocratic leadership is best when decisions must be made quickly.
12.	A	PDM is an approach commonly used to implement CPM. It is also referred to as AON. Either response would be correct.
13.	A	Rolling Wave Planning provides detailed plans for known activities, and develops planning packages for less defined activities.
14.	B	Option B is best. Option A is partially correct. Risks can also impact a project positively. Option C is incorrect. Risk is not always an unknown. However, it is always uncertain. Option D is not totally correct. Risks can occur during all Process Groups.

15.	D	Agile requirements are included in a Product Backlog, which consists of prioritized and estimated User Stories.
16.	C	The Schedule Management Plan is a "How To" document defining scheduling methods, schedule tools, and schedule configuration management procedures.
17.	C	Reward and Expert are top two power sources.
18.	B	An organization's structure, systems, and culture including standards and regulations are Enterprise Environmental Factors.
19.	B	Finish-to-Finish: Successor activity cannot finish until Predecessor activity finishes.
20.	D	Open ended activities lack a predecessor, successor, or both.
21.	A	ADM uses Finish-to-Start relationship only.
22.	A	Starting a successor activity before completion of the predecessor is a lead.
23.	B	Communications channels are calculated $((n*(n-1))/2$. Solution: $(8*7)/2 = 28$.
24.	D	Define Milestones identifies events or points in time that must be met to achieve project goals and objectives.
25.	B	Critical path cannot be evaluated until completion of Determine Durations.
26.	B	The math: $(100 + 100 + 50 + 50 + 0)/500 = 60\%$. Completed activities receive a score of 100. Started Work Packages receive a score of 50. Not started scores 0.
27.	A	Bar charts are best option for management presentations.
28.	B	This is a negative float scenario. Answer is -3.
29.	C	Formula: Value of Work Remaining/Value of Budget Remaining. $2,000/$1,500 = 1.33$.
30.	B	One-point estimating probability is approximately 15% correct.
31.	D	RBS is completed after sequence activities step.
32.	C	Option C is correct. Questionnaires soliciting expert input matches Delphi Technique approach.
33.	C	Bottom Up estimation is best for complex and/or ambiguous projects.
34.	D	Internal dependencies are within team's ability to control.
35.	A	Control Quality is the first step in the closure process.

36.	B	Work Authorization Systems provide procedures dictating how and when work can progress.
37.	D	Path convergence occurs when multiple activities flow into or out of a single activity.
38.	B	The Scope Statement is the most detailed version of scope.
39.	A	Calculation: (80% × $2,000) + (40% × $3,000) + (100% × $5,000) = $1,600 + $1,200 + $5,000 = $7,800.
40.	C	Beta distribution is the same as PERT. Calculation: ((1 × 6) + (4 × 11) + (1 × 22))/6 = 12.
41.	B	Bottom Up Estimating is best when a project type is new, or there are ambiguities that must be addressed.
42.	C	Formula: (10 × 9)/2 = 45.
43.	B	Supportive stakeholders agree with projects, but are not actively engaged.
44.	C	Critical path is longest path: BFDE or 14 days
45.	C	SPI = EV/PV. EV is $32,000 (40% × $80,000). PV is $40,000 (40% × $80,000). Calculation: $32,000/$40,000 = 0.8
46.	A	SV = EV – PV. Calculation: $32,000 - $40,000 = ($8,000).
47.	D	Fast tracking adds risk—use this technique to compress schedules. Changing network diagram logic means reducing scope—a viable option. Value analysis is a viable method of finding a cheaper way to do things—you are behind on budget. You have no resources to crash. Your CPI is .71. Not a viable option.
48.	C	Math: (0.3 × $2,000) + (0.6 × $8,000) = $5,400.

49.	A	The only weighted estimation method is PERT. Apply the formula (O +4ML +P)/6 = Estimate. Math: 144/6 = 24 Days.
50.	B	Resource Levelling balances out resources. If on critical path, time required to complete the project is often extended.
51.	B	Lessons Learned should be accomplished at end of each project phase. Lessons Learned may be conducted formally or informally, and document only events that occurred or are now occurring.
52.	B	Communications Management Plan documents who to share status/required reports with.
53.	A	Monte Carlo is used during Simulation.
54.	C	The Kick Off meeting presents a Project Management Plan to stakeholders for acceptance.
55.	D	Both Control Quality and Validate Scope use inspections to evaluate results.
56.	C	Validate Scope seeks to gain customer acceptance of deliverables once verified by Control Quality.
57.	C	Always use Three-Point averaging unless you are directed to use PERT or a weighted estimation method. Add three estimates together and divide by three to calculate average. (25 +16 +10 = 51/3 = 17)
58.	D	Communications blockers lead to conflict.
59.	B	E-mail is classified as Informal Written communications.
60.	A	Best means to identify stakeholders is begin with brainstorming followed by interviews.
61.	B	There are 5 paths: ABEH: 22, CDEH: 21, CDFI: 23, CDG: 20, ABEI: 25. Critical path is ABEI.
62.	D	Activity H is not on critical path. It has float.
63.	B	Adding J creates new critical path CJDFI: 26 Days.
64.	C	Path ABEI is 25 days. It is "Near Critical Path."
65.	C	Fast tracking makes ABEI 20 Days. AB is completed at same time and requires 7 days.
66.	C	Push communications are not a technology factor impacting communications.
67.	A	Stakeholder Register is an input to schedule planning. It is developed during Project Initiating.
68.	D	Option D defines Nominal Group Technique.

69.	D	Internal dependencies are precedence relationships between project activities within the team's control.
70.	A	A beta distribution is another way to refer to PERT or weighted estimation method. PERT Formula: (P +4ML + O)/6.
71.	B	Two Resource Optimization methods are Resource Levelling and Resource Smoothing.

Refer to tables below for questions 72 – 77.

Activity	% Complete	Value	EV	Actual Costs	PV
A	100%	$2,000	$2,000	$2,000	
B	70%	$4,000	$2,800	$3,000	
C	40%	$3,000	$1,200	$1,400	
D	0%	$2,000	$0	$200	
E	0%	$4,000	$0	$0	
TOTAL		$15,000	$6,000	$6,600	$7,500

Calculations	
SV	($1,500)
CV	($600)
SPI	0.80
CPI	0.91
EAC	$16,500

72.	C	EV = $6,000. Multiply each Activity % × Value to determine individual activity EV. Sum for total.
73.	D	BAC is sum total of values = $15,000.
74.	B	SPI = EV/PV. PV = 50% × BAC ($15,000) = $7,500.
75.	C	SPI is less than 1.0.
76.	B	Cannot crash. You are over budget.
77.	A	EAC = BAC/CPI = $16,500.
78.	D	The Communications Management Plan shares how, when, and with whom communications are executed.

Refer to the diagram below for responses to questions 79 – 82.

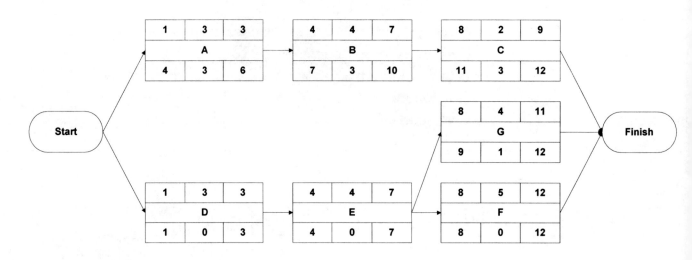

79.	C	Critical path: 12 days.
80.	B	Activity B: 3 days float.
81.	A	Activity G LS: 12 days.
82.	B	Activity C EF: 9 days.
83.	B	Autocratic leadership is not likely to be effective when team is storming.
84.	D	Schedules are number one cited source of potential conflict.
85.	B	Procurement Audits analyze the overall procurement process to determine future contractual performance improvements.
86.	A	Know what each box in this symbol represents. ES = 8, Duration = 6, EF = 13, LS = 10, Float = 2, and LF = 15.
87.	C	Scenario defines Work Performance Data. Work Performance Data is used to create Work Performance Information.
88.	C	CV = $400. SV = $200. SPI = 2200/2000 = 1.1. Only CPI is correct. 2200/1800 = 1.22.
89.	D	Responses to negative float include changing network/schedule logic, fast tracking, crashing, and obtaining authority to change schedules.
90.	A	Code of Account Identifier is the numbering system used to identify WBS activities.
91.	B	Analogous uses information from similar past projects for estimating. Analogous is also categorized as Expert or Top Down estimating.
92.	D	Critical Path CDFEI = 22 Days
93.	C	Near Critical Path ABFEI = 21 Days

94.	A	Activity A is not on critical path and has float.
95.	B	CDHJ = 22 Days. Two critical paths.
96.	A	The Stakeholder Register provides key information on project stakeholders including customers.
97.	C	Transfer and share are risk strategies used when 3rd parties are required. Use Transfer for threats. Use Share for opportunities.
98.	B	The IFB best matches a Fixed Price contract.
99.	D	Three point estimating provides either a triangular or beta distribution. Triangular distribution is an average. Beta distribution is weighted.
100.	B	Discretionary dependencies are used to reduce risk. They can be fast tracked.
101.	D	Issues logs are used to manage stakeholders. They are developed during the Manage Stakeholder Engagement process.
102.	B	PDM is the most common network diagramming method. It is also referred to as AON.
103.	C	Critical Chain Method uses buffers to guard against delays.
104.	A	A Forensic Schedule Analysis is a cause and effect review of a project used in legal proceedings.
105.	A	The Fixed Price family of contracts puts Cost Risk on the seller. Cost Reimbursement and Time and Material type contracts put Cost Risk on the buyer.

106.	D	Solution: • BAC is $60,000. • Project is 40% complete. EV is (40% × $60,000) = $24,000. • You planned to be 30% complete at this point. PV is (30% × $60,000) = $18,000. • AC is $25,000. Option A is incorrect. Project is not behind schedule. Calculate Schedule Variance (EV-PV). Result is +$6,000. Project is ahead of schedule. Option B is incorrect. Project is not ahead on budget. Calculate Cost Variance (EV-AC). Result is -$1,000. Project is behind on budget. Option C is incorrect. Schedule Variance (SV) is positive. Option D is correct. Cost Variance (CV) is negative.
107.	B	SPI is calculated EV/PV. Options C and D are CV and SV results. Option A is the CPI (EV/AC). Option B is correct. SPI = ($24,000/$18,000) = 1.33.
108.	C	Development of Issues Logs and implementation of strategy to move stakeholders to desired states occur during Manage Stakeholder Engagement.
109.	D	Communications technology factors include urgency of need for information, technology availability, ease of use, sensitivity and confidentiality of information, and project environment.
110.	D	Market Research is used in Plan Procurement Management to complete a Procurement Management Plan.
111.	A	Fast track discretionary dependencies only. Another term for discretionary dependencies is "Soft or Preferred Logic".
112.	B	Parametric matches unit × time to determine estimates.
113.	A	BAC for four weeks is $100,000. Week 2 is 50% times $100,000, or $50,000.
114.	A	Project is behind schedule (SPI .93) and ahead on budget (1.07). Best option is to crash. Crashing improves schedule performance when there is a budget surplus. Fast tracking addresses problems, but increases risk.

115.	B	Communications blockers generally result in conflict.
116.	D	Hertzberg is responsible for the motivational theory dealing with hygiene factors and motivating agents.
117.	D	Backward pass is a CPM process revealing late start and late finish dates.
118.	A	Follow change management steps. Log and evaluate all changes, develop options, and present changes for approval or rejection.
119.	D	Yield to customer needs whenever possible when there are scope questions.
120.	D	Laissez-Faire is a leadership style best explained as hands-off. All other styles listed involve interaction.
121.	C	The Quality Management Plan defines Quality Assurance methods to ensure standards are met and quality metrics driving the project.
122.	A	Do not evaluate ideas during brainstorming. Goal of brainstorming is to solicit ideas you evaluate later.
123.	B	Supporting Leadership Style is best during Norming and Performing stages of the Tuckman Model.
124.	A	Keep Satisfied is best when dealing with stakeholders with High Power and Low Interest.
125.	D	Delphi Technique helps attain expert input and mitigates stakeholder fears.
126.	C	Projectized structure allows project managers high levels of authority and independence.
127.	A	Cultural and Social environment impacts stakeholder acceptance of projects.
128.	B	Salience model classifies by power, urgency, and legitimacy.

Team Member	A	B	C	
Skill/Efficiency Level	0.8	1	0.75	
Availability	100%	60%	80%	
PI	0.80	0.60	0.60	0.67

10 Day Activity	12.5	16.67	16.67	
All Working	5			

129.	C	(Note table above) Always assume a single resource with a skill level of 1 and 100% capacity completes task as scheduled. This scenario is 10 days. Answer: 5 Days. $(10/(0.8 + 0.6 + 0.6)) = 10/2 = 5$
130.	B	$10/0.8 = 12.5$ Days
131.	A	$.75 \times .80 = .60$
132.	C	Tool to consolidate ideas through individual brainstorming sessions into a single map reflecting commonality and differences in understanding and generating new ideas is definition of an Idea/Mind Map.
133.	B	Plan Stakeholder Management. Control Stakeholder Engagement is when you review strategies and adjust as required.
134.	C	Monte Carlo is a Simulation tool.
135.	D	False picture of potential float, reduced potential to identify risk, and obscuring logical relationships are generally results of open ended activities.
136.	A	Sensitivity Analysis uses several What-If scenarios to calculate potential results. This modeling technique helps determine risks with greatest impact on a project.
137.	B	Communications model shows why communications is challenging. It is not likely included in a Communications Management Plan.
138.	C	Claims Administration clauses provide formal guidance for identifying and processing contract issues.
139.	A	Project is behind schedule--ahead on budget. Best strategy is crash. (EV = 50% × $4,000 = $2,000)
140.	A	Stakeholder Management Plan lists strategies to move stakeholders from current to desired commitment levels.
141.	D	CV is positive. CV = EV – AC. $2,500 - $2,250 = $250.
142.	C	SV = EV – PV. In this scenario, change the formula to PV = EV – SV. Math: $12,000 - ($2,000) = $14,000.
143.	D	This symbol is used in CPM to show a variety of scheduling information about an activity. Correct response is float = 2 days.
144.	D	LF: 7 days.
145.	B	WBS defines all activities and Work Packages to complete a project. You need a WBS to effectively perform Project Time Management.
146.	A	The Activity Calendar is used for actual schedule calculations.

147.	B	Code of Account Identifier is the specific numeric identifier assigned to an individual Work Package in a WBS.
148.	C	All responses are important. Number one goal is influence factors that cause change.
149.	B	Level 3 reports best meet this need.
150.	D	This is a crashing scenario. Crashing is a Compression Technique, poses risk of increased costs, and near critical path creation.

APPENDIX C: Acronyms

Acronym	Definition
AC	Actual Costs
ADM	Activity Diagramming Method
AOA	Activity on Arrow
AON	Activity on Node
BAC	Budget at Completion
CCB	Change Control Board
CPI	Cost Performance Index
CPM	Critical Path Method
CR	Cost Reimbursement
CSAT	Customer Satisfaction
CV	Cost Variance
D	Duration
DMAIC	Define, Measure, Analyze, Improve, Control
EAC	Estimate at Completion
EF	Early Finish
EMV	Expected Monetary Value
ES	Early Start
ETC	Estimate to Completion
EV	Earned Value
EVM	Earned Value Management
F	Float
FF	Finish to Finish
FMEA	Failure Modes and Effect Analysis
FP	Fixed Price
FS	Finish to Start
IFB	Invitation for Bid
IMP	Integrated Master Plan
IMS	Integrated Master Schedule
ISO	International Organization for Standardization
KISS	Keep it Short and Sweet

Acronym	Definition
LF	Late Finish
LOE	Level of Effort
LS	Late Start
OBS	Organizational Breakdown Structure
OSHA	Occupational Safety and Health Administration
PDCA	Plan, Do, Check, Act
PDM	Precedence Diagramming Method
PERT	Program Evaluation Review Technique
PMB	Performance Measurement Baseline
PMBOK®	Project Management Body of Knowledge
PMI®	Project Management Institute
PMI-SP®	PMI Scheduling Professional
RBS	Resource Breakdown Structure
RFP	Request for Proposal
RFQ	Request for Quotation
SF	Start to Finish
SIPOC	Supplier, Input, Process, Output, Customer
SMART	Specific, Measureable, Achievable, Relevant, Target Driven
SME	Subject Matter Expert
SOW	Statement of Work
SPI	Schedule Performance Index
SS	Start to Start
SV	Schedule Variance
SWOT	Strengths, Weaknesses, Opportunities, Threats
TCPI	To Complete Performance Index
TM	Time and Material
VAC	Variance at Completion
WBS	Work Breakdown Structure

APPENDIX D: Glossary of Terms and Index

Term	Chapter	Definition
Accept	7	Response to negative or positive risk. No action prescribed should risk occur.
Activity Calendar	4	Defines working and non-working times. Replaces Project Calendar for actual schedule calculations.
Activity Network Diagram	3	Diagram of project activities. Shows most realistic path and schedule for project completion. Graphically shows tasks, dependencies, and critical activities.
Activity on Arrow (AOA)	1	Another term for ADM.
Activity on Node (AON)	1	Another term for PDM.
Actual Costs (AC)	4	Used in EVM. Budget spent to date.
Affinity Diagramming	7	Method to categorize options through group brainstorming.
Agile Methodology	1	Form of CPM planning. Determine what is produced in a given iteration. Focuses on providing value quickly.

Term	Chapter	Definition
Alternatives Analysis	3	Determine most efficient means to complete a project using resources available.
Analogous Estimating	3	Uses actual durations of previous, similarly scheduled activities or projects as basis for time estimates. Also called Expert or Top Down.
Arrow Diagramming Method (ADM)	1	Relationships between activities represented by circles connected by one or more arrows. Uses dummy tasks.
Assumption	2	Something believed to be true but yet to be validated.
Avoid	7	Response to negative risk. Eliminate a negative cause.
Backward Pass	1	Form of CPM determining late start and late finish dates.
Bar Chart	3	Project presentation using bars to share a project schedule. Often used in management presentations.
Bias	7	Factors that may skew a risk assessment to include motivational (intentional) and cognitive (perceptions).
Bottom Up Estimating	3	Method of estimating. Determines costs and time requirements for each Work Package. Aggregate all estimates.

Term	Chapter	Definition
Budget at Completion (BAC)	4	Used in EVM. Dollar value of total project.
Buffer	2	Critical Chain Method adding time to account for risk.
Change Control Board (CCB)	4	Board consisting of Project Sponsor/senior leadership convened to review and approve/reject change requests.
Change Log	4	Log to track and manage project changes.
Claims Administration Clause	5	Guidance on how buyers and sellers process and communicate contract issues.
Closing	5	Fifth Process Group. Transition deliverables to operations, close contracts, and gain acceptance.
Code of Account Identifier	2	Unique numeric designator for each activity/Work Package in WBS.
Communications Blocker	6	Limits effectiveness of communications. Sometimes referred as "Noise" factors.
Communications Channels	6	Number of individual conversations occurring within a team based on number of team members.

Term	Chapter	Definition
Communications Management Plan	2, 6	Plan establishes project communications expectations and rhythm.
Communications Model	6	Model showing flow of communications between sender and receiver. Points out communications challenges.
Compression Techniques	4	Methods to accelerate project schedules or prevent delays on critical path. Common methods include fast tracking and crashing.
Configuration Management	2	Manage change to project's functional and physical characteristics.
Conflict Management	7	Manage and control conflict. Methods include collaborate, compromise, withdraw, smoothing, and forcing.
Constraint	2	Situations/events limiting a project such as regulations, dependencies, economic conditions, capacity, etc.
Contingency Plan	7	Primary action planned to respond to a risk.
Contingency Reserves	3	Funds set aside to address known risks.
Corrective Change	4	Change requests to correct actual problems.

Term	Chapter	Definition
Cost Performance Index (CPI)	4	Calculation of EVM. Shows whether you are ahead of, equal to, or behind on budget. Shows percentage.
Cost Variance (CV)	4	Calculation of EVM. Shows whether you are ahead of, equal to, or behind on budget. Shows dollar amount.
Crashing	3	Use resources from Work Packages with float and apply them to Work Packages on critical path to prevent delays.
Critical Activity	3	Activity critical to project success. May be high risk. May not be on critical path.
Critical Chain Method	1, 3	Scheduling method considering impact of risk to schedules by applying buffers.
Critical Path	1, 3	Project Network Diagram path of longest duration. Measure of how long the project will take.
Critical Path Method (CPM)	1, 3	Scheduling method determining float and critical path activities using forward and backward passes.
Cultural and Social Environment	7	How project impacts people and buy-in.
Decomposition	2, 3	Breaking down WBS into levels.

Term	Chapter	Definition
Deliverable	2	Measurable product or service from a project.
Delphi Technique	7	Technique to attain input eliminating apprehension and fear. Inputs solicited in a manner where submitters remain anonymous.
Discretionary Dependency	3	Included during schedule planning to reduce risk. Can be broken.
DMAIC	2	Define, Measure, Analyze, Improve, Control.
Dummy Task	1	Used in ADM. Represents a dependency between tasks. Not an actual activity.
Earned Value (EV)	1	Used in EVM. Dollar value of work accomplished.
Earned Value Management (EVM)	1. 4	Common method used to show current schedule and cost status for a project.
Enhance	7	Response to positive risk. Prescribes actions to either increase the possibility of a risk occurring, or heighten positive impact if it occurs.
Enterprise Environmental Factors	2	Organization's structure, systems, culture, standards and regulations impacting a project.

Term	Chapter	Definition
Estimate at Completion (EAC)	4	EVM calculation. Shows final budget at completion if CV and CPI trends continue.
Estimate to Complete (ETC)	4	Cost to complete a project from predetermined point in time.
Executing	7	Third step in the project management framework. Implement Project Management Plan as written.
Expectancy Theory	7	Motivational theory. Links effort and performance to rewards.
Expert Judgement	2	SME providing input during project planning.
Exploit	7	Response to positive risk. Accentuate and enable a positive cause.
External Dependency	3	Dependencies generally driven by external factors as policy, regulation, compliance, law, etc.
Externalities	4	External dependencies or constraints impacting/resulting from a project.
Fallback Plan	7	Secondary action planned to respond to a risk should Contingency Plan prove to be unfeasible or ineffective.

Term	Chapter	Definition
Fast Tracking	3	Eliminate discretionary dependencies and start Work Packages simultaneously.
Feeding Buffer	1	Add at merger point of critical and non-critical path to address uncertainties identified during project planning.
Finish-to-Finish	3	Successor activity cannot finish until Predecessor activity has finished.
Finish-to-Start	3	Successor activity cannot start until Predecessor activity has finished.
Float	1, 3	Capability to extend time required to complete an activity without impacting critical path.
FMEA	7	Failure Modes and Effect Analysis.
Forensic Schedule Analysis	5	Performed retrospectively to determine true cause and impact of schedule delays. May be used for legal proceedings.
Formal Communications	6	Correspondence meant for public consumption or matter of record.
Forward Pass	1	Form of CPM determining early start and early finish dates.

Term	Chapter	Definition
Free Float	3	Time an activity early finish date can be delayed without impacting a successor activities early start date.
Functional	7	Organizational Structure. Traditional "silo" model. Employees grouped by specialty.
Functional Manager	2	Managers providing authorized personnel resources needed for a project.
Hammock Activity	3	See Level of Effort (LOE) Activity.
Hertzberg's Theory	7	Hygiene's do not motivate but can demotivate. Motivators lift us up.
Idea Mapping	7	Method to categorize options through individual brainstorming.
Informal Communications	6	Correspondence not meant for public consumption or matter of record.
Initiating	7	First step in project management framework. Develop Project Charter and Stakeholder Register.
Inspection	4, 5	Perform Quality Control and Validate Scope for a project.

Term	Chapter	Definition
Instance	1	Copy of the schedule model. Multiple instances are completed as a project progresses and schedule models change.
Integrated Change Control (ICC)	4	Process to manage project change.
Interactive Communications	6	Two or more parties; multi-directional exchange of information.
Internal Dependency	3	Dependency within team's control.
International and Political Environment	7	Knowledge of applicable laws and people's ulterior motives.
Interview	7	Method to gain expert input. Start with prepared questions--then spontaneous.
Issue	6	Question or problem impacting a team member. Risk that occurred.
Issue Log	6	Logs developed to track issues.
Iteration (Sprint)	1	Period of time where a set of Agile requirements are developed and presented.

Term	Chapter	Definition
Kick-Off Meeting	3	Meeting to present completed Project Management Plan to stakeholders to gain acceptance.
Known Risks	7	Risks identified and documented on a Risk Register.
Lag	3	Delay start of successor activity after completion of predecessor activity.
Lead	3	Implement successor activity prior to completion of predecessor activity.
Leadership Styles	7	Include directive, facilitative, coaching, supporting, consensus building, consultative, and autocratic.
Leading	6	Level of commitment designator. Stakeholder supportive and actively engaged in project.
Lessons Learned	5	Analyze what went well, what could improve, and recommend improvement changes over course of the project.
Level of Effort (LOE) Activity	3	Activity designated to support other activities or entire project. Duration based on total duration of all activities supported. Sometimes called Hammock Activity.
Management Reserves	3	Funds set aside to address unknown risks.

Term	Chapter	Definition
Mandatory Dependency	3	Dependencies integral to project's deliverable development. Cannot be broken.
Maslow	7	Five-step hierarchy of needs.
Matrix	7	Organizational Structure. Combines Functional and Projectized.
Milestone	2, 3	Point of time or event driving project schedule development.
Milestone Chart	3	Project presentation showing major milestones necessary to complete a project.
Mitigate	7	Response to negative risk. Prescribes actions to reduce possibility of risk occurring, or lesson negative impact.
Monitor and Controlling	7	Fourth step in project management framework. Ensure deliverables produced as planned. Take corrective action if variances identified.
Monte Carlo	3	Simulation tool. Determines probabilities of meeting project cost and schedule objectives.
Near Critical Path	4	A path in a project network diagram close in duration to critical path.

Term	Chapter	Definition
Negative Risk	7	Potential threat that may negatively impact scope, time, and costs.
Neutral	6	Level of commitment designator. Stakeholder yet to determine level of support.
Noise	6	See Communications Blockers.
Nominal Group Technique	7	Method to gain consensus. Brainstorm, then rank options.
Non-Verbal Communications	6	55% of communications. Not what you say or write.
One-Point Estimating	2	Estimation considering most likely estimate only.
Open Ended Activity	2	Activities lacking a predecessor, successor activity or both. Obscures logical relationships between activities, creates false picture of potential float, and reduces potential to identify risks.
Organizational Breakdown Structure (OBS)	2	Hierarchical organizational chart depicting the top-down organizational model for a firm.
Organizational Process Assets	2	Includes organizational policies and procedures, standard project management tools/templates, and historical information as Lessons Learned.

Term	Chapter	Definition
Paralingual	6	Tone of voice reveals thoughts and feelings.
Parametric Estimating	3	Estimation method multiplies units × time/cost to determine estimates.
PDCA	2	Plan, Do, Check, Act
Performance Measurement Baseline (PMB)	3	Approved plan for accomplishing all project work. Basis for measures.
PERT	3	Form of three-point estimating. Weights optimistic, most likely and pessimistic estimates to calculate estimates. Also called Beta Distribution.
Physical Environment	7	How project is impacted by surrounding environment.
Planned Value (PV)	4	Used in EVM. Depicts dollar value of work planned to accomplish by a certain timeframe.
Planning	7	Second step in project management framework. Complete planning and gain approval and acceptance of Project Management Plan.
Planning Packages	2	Activities planned at a high level in Rolling Wave Planning.

Term	Chapter	Definition
Post Mortem	5	Same as Lessons Learned.
Power	7	Methods used to influence others. Includes formal, reward, expert, penalty, and referent.
Power and Interest Grid	6	Classify stakeholders by power, and interest.
Pre-Baseline	7	Shows Project Charter was approved by Sponsor. Allows project to move into Planning.
Precedence Diagramming Method (PDM)	1, 3	Schedule diagramming technique using boxes or nodes to show how project activities are logically grouped.
Predecessor Activity	2	Activity on a Project Network Diagram that occurs before a successor activity.
Pre-Mortem	7	Identify potential risks before a project begins.
Presentation	1	Specific outputs from the schedule model used to communicate key data for analysis, course correction, decision making, etc.
Preventative Change	4	Change requests submitted to prevent potential problems.

Term	Chapter	Definition
Probability and Impact Assessment	7	Determine risk probability × impact to determine risk score.
Probability Risk Matrix	7	Matrix rating risk levels of urgency based on risk score.
Procurement Audit	5	Formal review of contract deliverables conducted at end of project. Evaluates total procurement process.
Procurement Management Plan	7	Document sharing end-to-end procurement strategy to support a project.
Product Backlog	1	Documents Agile requirements in the form of User Stories.
Productivity Index	2	Measure of resource's ability to accomplish project work based on skills and capacity.
Progress Reporting Methods	4	Methods used to determine EV using 50/50, 20/80, or 0/100 rules.
Progressive Elaboration	2	Gradual definition of scope over course of a project. Scope defined at a high level early in a project and "elaborated" or more detailed as project planning progresses.
Project	1	Projects are temporary, unique, and defined through progressive elaboration.

Term	Chapter	Definition
Project Buffer	1	Add time to end of the project to account for a variety of uncertainties identified during project planning.
Project Change Log	7	Document to log and track status of project change requests.
Project Change Management Process	7	Process to manage project change requests. Log change, evaluate, determine options, make recommendations, and share decisions.
Project Charter	2	Important first step when project is born. Defines, at a high-level, what the project will deliver.
Project Management Body of Knowledge (*PMBOK®*)	1	Published by PMI. Provides generally recognized practices in project management and shares common vocabulary.
Project Manager	1	Responsible for project deliverables and managing expectations. Controls project processes.
Project Network Diagram	2, 3	Uses project WBS to lay out chronological plan to effectively complete all activities.
Project Scope Statement	3	Most detailed version of scope.
Projectized	7	Organizational Structure. Managed and consisting of project managers directly reporting to leadership.

Term	Chapter	Definition
Prompt List	7	Generic list of risk categories.
Pull Communications	6	Information available to stakeholders at their discretion; i.e. share point or web site.
Pure Logic Project Network Diagram	3	Project Network Diagram showing only logic and no duration.
Push Communications	6	Communications with no certification information was received or understood.
Qualitative Risk Analysis	7	Method of qualifying risks by assigning probability and impact values to determine a risk score.
Quality Assurance (QA)	4, 5	Activities conducted during Executing to ensure team is following the project plan, standards, processes, etc. Goal is to prevent problems.
Quality Audit	4, 5	Performance of Quality Assurance for the project.
Quality Control (QC)	5	Activities conducted during Monitor and Control to ensure deliverables conform to requirements. Goal is to correct problems.
RACI	7	Methodology to define particular stakeholder role using Responsible, Accountable, Consult, Inform designators.

Term	Chapter	Definition
Residual Risk	7	Risk remaining after risk response was undertaken. Generally identified during Risk Audit.
Resistant	6	Level of commitment designator. Stakeholder doesn't support the project.
Resource Breakdown Structure	2	Tool allowing you to effectively estimate resources required to complete project work.
Resource Buffer	1	Additional resources required to complete a project activity due to uncertainties identified during planning.
Resource Calendar	3	Document when project resources are required.
Resource Constrained Schedule	3	Plan a schedule considering resource constraints.
Resource Levelling	3	Resource Optimization Technique. Balance out resources on critical path. Often extends schedule.
Resource Optimization Techniques	3	Use of Resource levelling or Resource Smoothing to balance out project human resource tasking.
Resource Smoothing	3	Resource Optimization Technique. Balance out resources on non-critical path. Generally doesn't extend schedule but reduces float.

Term	Chapter	Definition
Retrospective	1	Evaluate performance of team at conclusion of an Agile iteration. Define and implement improvements.
Risk	7	Potential event that may impact a project either positively or negatively.
Risk Audit	7	Review of a risk response. Reviews how response went, and annotates results for Lessons Learned.
Risk Breakdown Structure	3, 7	Hierarchical breakout of potential risks by category used in risk identification.
Risk Management Plan	7	Provides guidance and information to members of the risk management team. A "how to" manage project risk overview.
Risk Metalanguage	7	Process to identify and document risks. Uses cause-event-impact methodology.
Risk Owner	7	Team member assigned to monitor and manage a given risk. Initiates responses if required.
Risk Reassessment	7	Periodic review of project risks. Generally accomplished weekly.
Risk Register	3, 7	Tool to identify, document and manage project risks.

Term	Chapter	Definition
Risk Trigger	7	Any action or indicator a risk is about to occur. Allows for early initiation of risk responses.
Rolling Wave Planning	1	Plan in detail activities known and understood. Delay planning on successor activities until more information is understood.
Salience Model	6	Classifying stakeholders by power, legitimacy, and urgency.
Schedule Baseline	2	Approved and accepted schedule documented in Project Management Plan.
Schedule Compression Techniques	3	Fast tracking or crashing to compress schedules.
Schedule Management Plan	2, 3	Process driven "how to" guide. Defines scheduling methods, applicable tools, and details of the schedule model to include required presentations.
Schedule Model	1, 2	Applies selected scheduling method and uses scheduling tool to produce various schedule model copies, referred to as instances.
Schedule Network Analysis	1, 3	Various techniques used to produce a project schedule.
Schedule Performance Index (SPI)	4	Calculation of EVM. Shows whether you are ahead of, equal to, or behind schedule as percentage.

Term	Chapter	Definition
Schedule Variance (SV)	4	Calculation of EVM. Shows whether you are ahead of, equal to, or behind schedule as dollar amount.
Scheduling Tool	1	Automated application to perform schedule network analysis.
Scope	3	Definition of product or service a project provides.
Scope Baseline	3	Approved and accepted Scope Statement, WBS, and WBS Dictionary.
Scope Creep	7	Process of adding scope without going through a formal change process.
Settlement	5	Negotiated settlement of a contract when terminated early, or disputes or claims are evident.
Share	7	Response to positive risk. Find third party to address positive risks.
Simulation	3	Uses Monte Carlo to determine schedule and cost probabilities.
SMART	2	Analyze requirements to ensure they are specific, measurable, attainable, relevant, and target driven.

Term	Chapter	Definition
Sponsor	3	Responsible for approving project, allocating funding, and providing project manager authority.
Staffing Management Plan	7	Outlines when human resources are required to support the project.
Stakeholder	3, 6	Any individual interested or impacted by a project.
Stakeholder Change	4	Change request submitted by any project stakeholder.
Stakeholder Management Plan	6	Tool to classify stakeholder levels of commitment, and develop strategies ensuring commitment at proper levels.
Stakeholder Register	6	Defines project stakeholders and roles.
Start-to-Finish	3	Successor activity cannot finish until predecessor activity has started.
Start-to-Start	3	Successor activity cannot start until predecessor activity has started.
Successor Activity	2	Activity on Project Network Diagram occurring after a predecessor.

Term	Chapter	Definition
Supportive	6	Level of commitment designator. Stakeholder agrees with project.
SWOT Analysis	7	Method to identify risks. Identify strengths leading to opportunities and weaknesses leading to threats.
Theory X and Y	7	Two diverse management styles.
Three Needs Theory	7	People are motivated by achievement, affiliation, and empowerment.
Three-Point Estimating	3	Method of estimation considering optimistic, most likely, and pessimistic scenarios. Common methods are averaging and PERT.
Three-Point Estimating Averaging	3	Sum optimistic, most likely and pessimistic estimates. Use average as time estimate. Also called Triangular Distribution.
To Complete Performance Index (TCPI)	4	Level of effort required to complete a project based on BAC or EAC.
Total Float	3	Amount of time an early start or early finish date can be delayed without impacting the late finish date for the entire project.
Transfer	7	Response to negative risk. Find third party to address a negative risk.

Term	Chapter	Definition
Transition Requirements	5	Plan for transition of project's product or service to operations after project is complete.
Tuckman Model	7	Model showing four stages a team goes through to achieve high performance. Steps include form, storm, norm, and perform.
Unaware	6	Level of commitment designator. Stakeholder not aware of project.
Unknown Risks	7	Risks not yet identified.
Urgent List	7	Risks with high risk score requiring most attention.
User Story	1	Primary Agile requirement. States role, need, value proposition, and acceptance criteria.
Validate Scope	5	Process when customers inspect and accept project deliverables.
Value Analysis	4	Find a cheaper way to achieve objectives.
Variance Analysis	2, 4	Monitoring planned versus actual project results and taking corrective actions as necessary.

Term	Chapter	Definition
Variance at Completion (VAC)	4	How much project finished over or under budget.
Watch List	7	Risks with a low risk score requiring least amount of attention.
What-If Scenario Analysis	3	Evaluate scenarios to determine impact on project objectives.
Work Authorization System	5	Rules dictating how and when a project may proceed from activity to activity.
Work Breakdown Structure (WBS)	2	Hierarchical breakout of project activities attained through decomposition.
Work Breakdown Structure Dictionary	2	Supplements WBS. Defines activity attributes to provide clarification of activities.
Work Package	2	Lowest level of WBS.
Work Performance Data	4	Raw information received during project Executing.
Work Performance Information	4	Create useable data during project Monitoring and Control from Work Performance Data.

Term	Chapter	Definition
Work Performance Reports	4	Generate project reports from Work Performance Information during Monitoring and Control.

CPSIA information can be obtained
at www.ICGtesting.com
Printed in the USA
FFOW01n1109081017
40673FF